Eyewitness
AZTEC

Peruvian mummy cloth

Aztec sacrificial knife

Mesoamerican farming tools

Ceremonial urn showing *Chaac*, Maya god of rain

Aztec ceramic flute

Marigolds, given as offerings to goddesses by the Aztecs

Moche vessel showing fisherman in boat

Peruvian silver portrait beaker

Olmec jade mask

Mortar and pestle
with chilli

Eyewitness
AZTEC

Written by
ELIZABETH BAQUEDANO

Photographed by
MICHEL ZABE

Aztec army commander

Toltec coyote
warrior inlaid with
mother-of-pearl

Aztec
skull mask

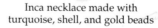

Inca necklace made with
turquoise, shell, and gold beads

DK

Warrior wearing feather headdress

LONDON, NEW YORK, MELBOURNE,
MUNICH and DELHI

Project editor Christine Webb
Art editor Andrew Nash
Managing editor Helen Parker
Managing art editor Julia Harris
Production Louise Barratt
Picture research Cynthia Hole
Researcher Céline Carez
Additional photography Andy Crawford, Dave Rudkin

PAPERBACK EDITION
Editors Barbara Berger, Laura Buller, Sue Nicholson
Editorial assistant John Searcy
Publishing director Beth Sutinis
Senior designer Tai Blanche
Designers Jessica Lasher, Diana Catherines, Rebecca Wright
Photo research Chrissy McIntyre
Art director Dirk Kaufman
DTP designers Milos Orlovic, Andy Hilliard
Production Ivor Parker, Angela Graef

This Eyewitness ® Guide has been conceived by
Dorling Kindersley Limited and Editions Gallimard

Hardback edition first published in Great Britain in 1993
This edition first published in Great Britain in 2006 by
Dorling Kindersley Limited,
80 Strand, London WC2R 0RL

2 4 6 8 10 9 7 5 3 1

Copyright © 1993, 2006 Dorling Kindersley Limited, London
A Penguin Company

A CIP catalogue record for this book is
available from the British Library.

ISBN-10 1 4053 1493 1
ISBN-13 978 1 4053 1493 0

Colour reproduction by Colourscan, Singapore
Printed in China by Toppan Printing Co., (Shenzhen) Ltd.

Discover more at
www.dk.com

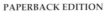

Zapotec jade
necklace

Toltec
warrior

Peruvian
feather fan

Mixtec head

Chancay
textile doll

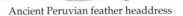

Ancient Peruvian feather headdress

Contents

Chacmool from
the Great Temple
of the Aztecs

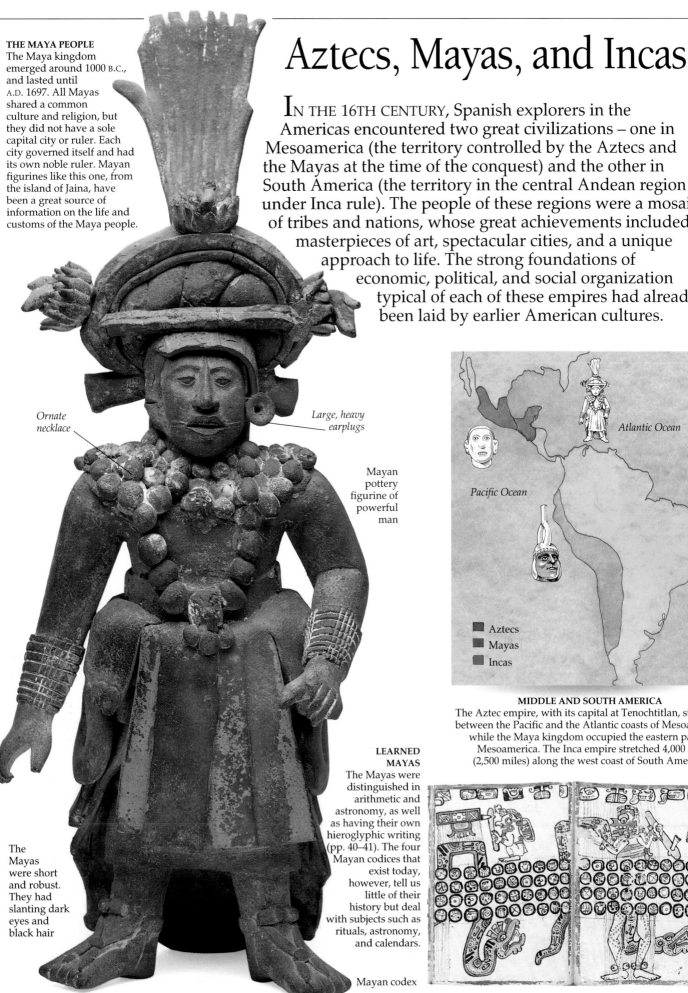

THE MAYA PEOPLE
The Maya kingdom emerged around 1000 B.C., and lasted until A.D. 1697. All Mayas shared a common culture and religion, but they did not have a sole capital city or ruler. Each city governed itself and had its own noble ruler. Mayan figurines like this one, from the island of Jaina, have been a great source of information on the life and customs of the Maya people.

I N THE 16TH CENTURY, Spanish explorers in the Americas encountered two great civilizations – one in Mesoamerica (the territory controlled by the Aztecs and the Mayas at the time of the conquest) – and the other in South America (the territory in the central Andean region under Inca rule). The people of these regions were a mosaic of tribes and nations, whose great achievements included masterpieces of art, spectacular cities, and a unique approach to life. The strong foundations of economic, political, and social organization typical of each of these empires had already been laid by earlier American cultures.

Ornate necklace

Large, heavy earplugs

Mayan pottery figurine of powerful man

The Mayas were short and robust. They had slanting dark eyes and black hair

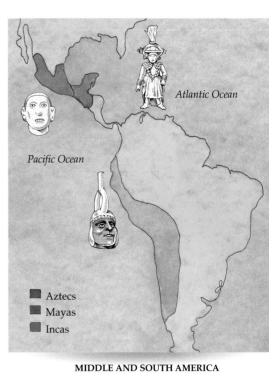

Atlantic Ocean

Pacific Ocean

■ Aztecs
■ Mayas
■ Incas

MIDDLE AND SOUTH AMERICA
The Aztec empire, with its capital at Tenochtitlan, stretch between the Pacific and the Atlantic coasts of Mesoameri while the Maya kingdom occupied the eastern part of Mesoamerica. The Inca empire stretched 4,000 km (2,500 miles) along the west coast of South America.

LEARNED MAYAS
The Mayas were distinguished in arithmetic and astronomy, as well as having their own hieroglyphic writing (pp. 40–41). The four Mayan codices that exist today, however, tell us little of their history but deal with subjects such as rituals, astronomy, and calendars.

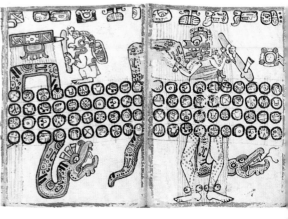

Mayan codex

THE FOUNDING OF TENOCHTITLAN

According to their mythology *Huitzilopochtli*, the tribal god of the Aztecs, promised to show his people a place where they were to settle and build their great capital Tenochtitlan. He told them to look for an eagle perched upon a cactus with a serpent in its beak. This first page of the Codex Mendoza (a book telling the history of the Aztecs) illustrates the foundation of Tenochtitlan in either 1325 or 1345. Mexico City is built on the same site.

INCA GOLD

The Incas excelled at working metals such as silver, copper, and gold (pp. 50–51). Female figures like this one have been found with Inca offerings to the gods.

Wooden beaker, or *kero*, with decoration of Inca man holding spear and shield

THE AZTECS

The Aztecs were a wandering tribe before they settled in the Valley of Mexico on swampy land in Lake Texcoco and founded Tenochtitlan. It grew in size and importance until it became the capital of the mighty Aztec empire. The Aztecs conquered many people, demanding tribute from them (pp. 26–27). The Aztecs were short and stocky, had brown skin and broad faces.

THE ANDEAN PEOPLE

The Inca empire became the most important state in the Andean highlands in 1438, when they conquered the area around the city Cuzco and made it their capital. The Incas conquered provinces and incorporated them into their empire. Due to their efficient administration system, they kept control over all their empire. The people of the Andean area were typically small, with straight black hair and brown skin.

Aztecs had thick black hair

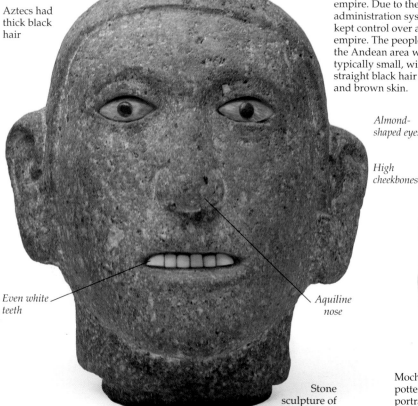

Even white teeth

Aquiline nose

Stone sculpture of Aztec head

Almond-shaped eyes

High cheekbones

Moche pottery portrait vessel

People of Mesoamerica

MESOAMERICA is one of two areas in the Americas (the other being the Central Andes) which had urban civilizations, or "high cultures", at the time of the Spanish conquest in 1519. The fact that Mesoamericans built spectacular pyramids and temples (pp. 30–31), had large markets (pp. 26–27), the ball-game (pp. 58–59), a sacred calendar, hieroglyphic writing (pp. 40–41), a group of gods (pp. 32–33), and practised human sacrifice (pp. 36–37) sets Mesoamerica apart from its neighbours. Mesoamerican cultural history is divided into three main periods: the Preclassic, the Classic, and the Postclassic, stretching from about 2000 B.C. until the Spanish conquest (pp. 62–63). During these periods Mesoamerica saw the rise and fall of many civilizations. The Olmecs were the dominant culture in the Preclassic period. The Classic period saw the rise of the mighty Teotihuacan culture, and the Mayas. The Postclassic period was one of militarism, strife, and warring empires like the Toltecs and the Aztecs.

WARRING AZTECS
At its height, the Aztec empire was strong and prosperous. Conquered areas were controlled by the powerful Aztec army. This illustration shows an army commander.

MAYAN RITUAL
Religion was the centre of every Mayan person's life. One of the major achievements of the Mayas was the construction of superb temples and other buildings to honour their gods. These were decorated with carvings such as this lintel showing a woman drawing blood from her tongue. Self-sacrifice was common throughout Mesoamerica.

MAP OF MESOAMERICA
Mesoamerica is both a geographical and a cultural region. At the time of the Spanish conquest it included what is now central and southern Mexico and the Peninsula of Yucatan, Guatemala, Belize, El Salvador, the westernmost part of Honduras, and a small part of Nicaragua and northern Costa Rica.

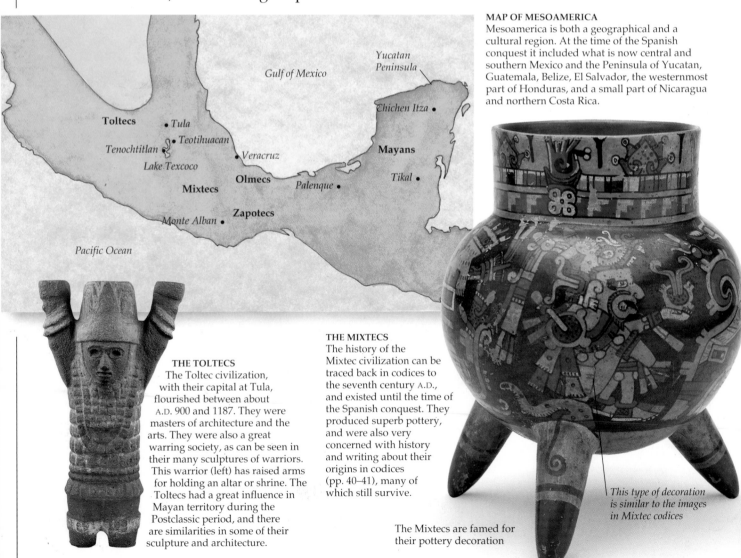

Yucatan Peninsula

Gulf of Mexico

Chichen Itza

Toltecs • Tula

• Teotihuacan

Tenochtitlan
Lake Texcoco • Veracruz **Mayans**

Mixtecs **Olmecs** Palenque Tikal

Monte Alban **Zapotecs**

Pacific Ocean

THE TOLTECS
The Toltec civilization, with their capital at Tula, flourished between about A.D. 900 and 1187. They were masters of architecture and the arts. They were also a great warring society, as can be seen in their many sculptures of warriors. This warrior (left) has raised arms for holding an altar or shrine. The Toltecs had a great influence in Mayan territory during the Postclassic period, and there are similarities in some of their sculpture and architecture.

THE MIXTECS
The history of the Mixtec civilization can be traced back in codices to the seventh century A.D., and existed until the time of the Spanish conquest. They produced superb pottery, and were also very concerned with history and writing about their origins in codices (pp. 40–41), many of which still survive.

This type of decoration is similar to the images in Mixtec codices

The Mixtecs are famed for their pottery decoration

8

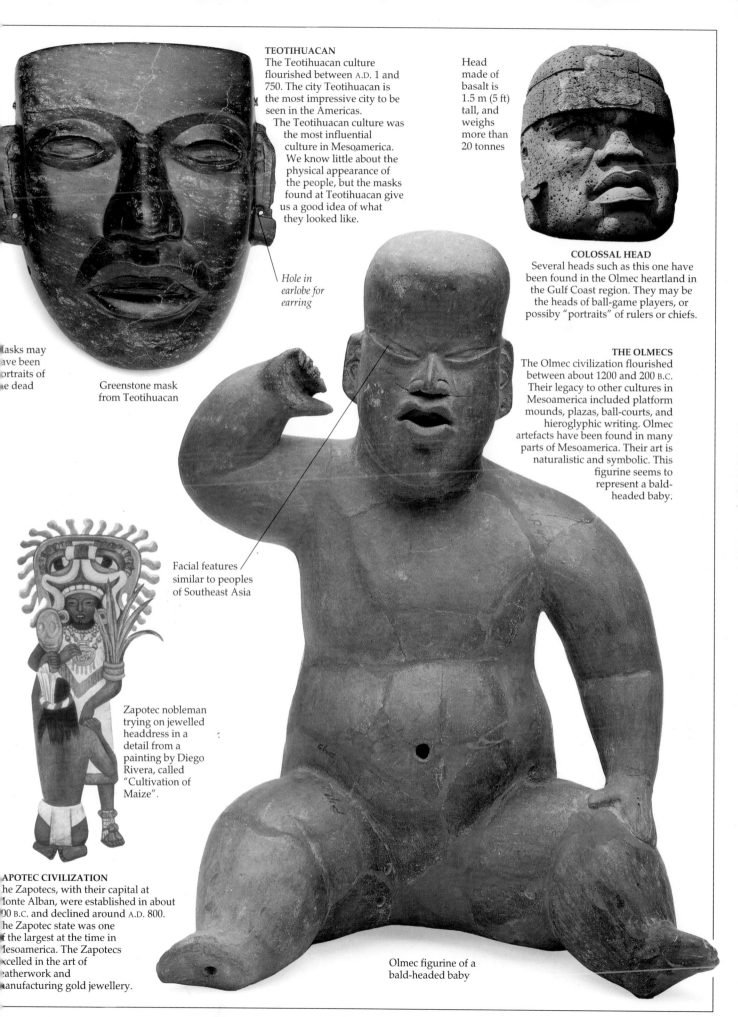

TEOTIHUACAN

The Teotihuacan culture flourished between A.D. 1 and 750. The city Teotihuacan is the most impressive city to be seen in the Americas.

The Teotihuacan culture was the most influential culture in Mesoamerica. We know little about the physical appearance of the people, but the masks found at Teotihuacan give us a good idea of what they looked like.

Head made of basalt is 1.5 m (5 ft) tall, and weighs more than 20 tonnes

Hole in earlobe for earring

Masks may have been portraits of the dead

Greenstone mask from Teotihuacan

COLOSSAL HEAD

Several heads such as this one have been found in the Olmec heartland in the Gulf Coast region. They may be the heads of ball-game players, or possiby "portraits" of rulers or chiefs.

THE OLMECS

The Olmec civilization flourished between about 1200 and 200 B.C. Their legacy to other cultures in Mesoamerica included platform mounds, plazas, ball-courts, and hieroglyphic writing. Olmec artefacts have been found in many parts of Mesoamerica. Their art is naturalistic and symbolic. This figurine seems to represent a bald-headed baby.

Facial features similar to peoples of Southeast Asia

Zapotec nobleman trying on jewelled headdress in a detail from a painting by Diego Rivera, called "Cultivation of Maize".

ZAPOTEC CIVILIZATION

The Zapotecs, with their capital at Monte Alban, were established in about 500 B.C. and declined around A.D. 800. The Zapotec state was one of the largest at the time in Mesoamerica. The Zapotecs excelled in the art of leatherwork and manufacturing gold jewellery.

Olmec figurine of a bald-headed baby

The Incas and their ancestors

BEFORE THE INCA empire reached its peak in South America, many Andean cultures had already laid the framework for its success. These cultures left no written records of their history, and all that is known of them comes from the study of their architecture, pottery, and the remains found in their graves. Archaeologists have identified separate periods of cultural growth culminating with the Incas. The first complex societies were formed in around 1800 B.C. Between this time and the rise of the Incas in the mid-15th century, various cultures emerged, gradually becoming highly organized civilizations with social structures, political and economic systems, specialized artisans, and a religion where many gods were worshipped. Along the desert coast of Peru there were civilized states such as the Nazca, the Moche, and the Chimu. In the highlands, the Huari and the Tiahuanaco were highly organized cultures. Between A.D. 1438 and 1534, all of these elements were brought together and improved on under the Inca empire.

NAZCA
The Nazca inhabited the southern coastal valleys of Peru from 300 B.C. to A.D. 600, and were well-known for their arts which included textiles and metalwork. However the hallmark of the Nazca civilization is its painted pottery, decorated with realistic and mythological scenes.

INCA NOBLES
The scenes painted on vessels and other objects help us learn more about Andean life and culture. For example, Inca nobles usually carried a lance, as this painting on a wooden beaker, or *kero*, shows.

Moche person of high status wearing headband with jaguar decoration and earplugs

TIAHUANACO
The Tiahuanaco empire from the Peruvian highlands flourished between about A.D. 500 and 650. It was a strong state with an impressive ceremonial centre.

Tiahuanaco pottery jaguar

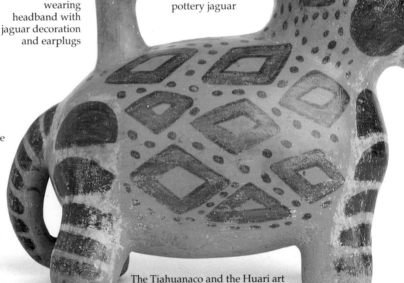

MOCHE
The Moche people flourished on the northern desert coast of Peru between about the time of Christ and A.D. 600. They were skilled goldsmiths and weavers, and remarkable potters. Their representations of people, plants, animals, and gods in a wide range of activities, give us an insight into their lives.

HUARI
The Huari (A.D. 500 to 900) were neighbours of the Tiahuanaco. Theirs was a highly organized state, with an advanced irrigation system and a distinctive architectural style. It expanded by conquering neighbouring areas. Many Huari ideas such as pottery techniques were adopted by other Andean cultures. Huari also had its own style of art. A common theme is an "angel" figure with wings such as this one.

The Tiahuanaco and the Huari art styles shared many of the same symbols, especially of the cat family

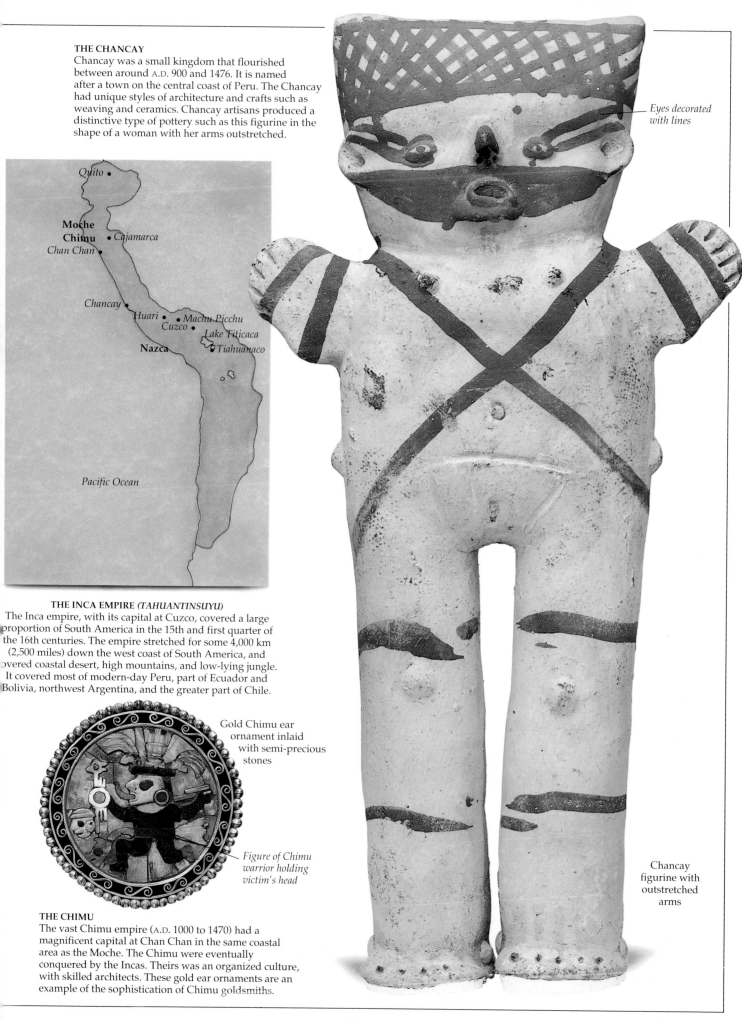

THE CHANCAY

Chancay was a small kingdom that flourished between around A.D. 900 and 1476. It is named after a town on the central coast of Peru. The Chancay had unique styles of architecture and crafts such as weaving and ceramics. Chancay artisans produced a distinctive type of pottery such as this figurine in the shape of a woman with her arms outstretched.

Eyes decorated with lines

Quito •

Moche
Chimu • Cajamarca
Chan Chan •

Chancay •

Huari • • Machu Picchu
Cuzco •
Lake Titicaca
Nazca • • Tiahuanaco

Pacific Ocean

THE INCA EMPIRE *(TAHUANTINSUYU)*

The Inca empire, with its capital at Cuzco, covered a large proportion of South America in the 15th and first quarter of the 16th centuries. The empire stretched for some 4,000 km (2,500 miles) down the west coast of South America, and covered coastal desert, high mountains, and low-lying jungle. It covered most of modern-day Peru, part of Ecuador and Bolivia, northwest Argentina, and the greater part of Chile.

Gold Chimu ear ornament inlaid with semi-precious stones

Figure of Chimu warrior holding victim's head

THE CHIMU

The vast Chimu empire (A.D. 1000 to 1470) had a magnificent capital at Chan Chan in the same coastal area as the Moche. The Chimu were eventually conquered by the Incas. Theirs was an organized culture, with skilled architects. These gold ear ornaments are an example of the sophistication of Chimu goldsmiths.

Chancay figurine with outstretched arms

Farming

AGRICULTURE WAS A VITAL PART of life in pre-Columbian times. Farmers used sophisticated methods of cultivation, and by the time of the Spanish conquest (p. 62) the ancient Americans were the greatest plant cultivators in the world. Maize from Mesoamerica and potatoes from the Andes (pp. 24–25) were some of their contributions to the European diet. Human labour was the vital ingredient in both regions, as there were no animals for carrying loads or ploughs in Mesoamerica. The Andean people had only the llama which could carry very small loads. Farming methods varied depending on the climate and geography of the area. For the Aztecs, the most productive crops were grown on the *chinampas*, plots of land built in swampy lakes.

FERTILE PLOTS
Crops of vegetables and flowers were grown on the fertile *chinampas*, as well as medicinal plants and herbs.

GODDESS OF AGRICULTURE
This incense burner (used to burn a resin called *copal*) represents an agricultural goddess. Agricultural goddesses were often adorned with a pleated paper fan, like this one.

BUILDING *CHINAMPAS* *below*
Chinampas were made by staking out narrow, rectangular strips in marshy lakes. Narrow canals were built between them for canoes to pass along. Each *chinampa* was built up with layers of thick water vegetation cut from the surface of the lake and mud from the bottom of the lake. They were piled up like mats to make the plots. Willow trees were planted around the edge of each *chinampa* to make it more secure.

Rich earth from the bottom of the lake was used as fertilizer

Maize

Long broad blade

FARMER'S TOOL
The digging stick, or *uictli*, was the essential farmer's tool. Digging sticks were used for various jobs, such as hoeing and planting.

PLANTING THE SEED
This illustration from the Codex Florentino shows an Aztec farmer planting maize using a digging stick.

DIGGING STICK
Digging sticks were made with the strongest and longest-lasting woods.

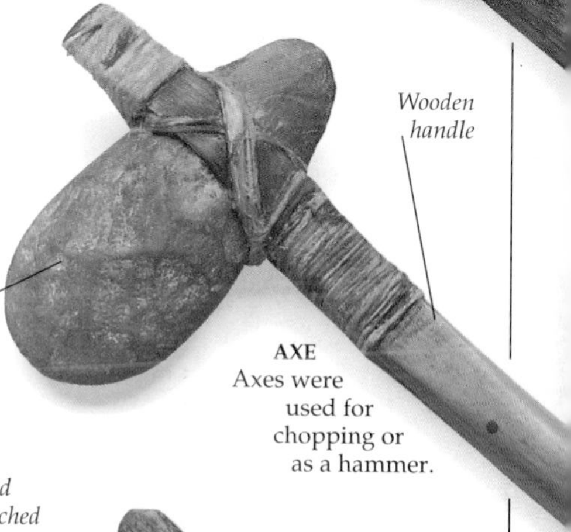

Wooden handle

Stone head

AXE
Axes were used for chopping or as a hammer.

Head attached to handle with cord

HARVEST TIME
Life in Mesoamerica and in the Andes revolved around the cycles of planting, cultivating, and harvesting crops such as maize.

MAIZE CROP
Maize was the staple food of the Mayans as well as the Aztecs. It is still an important crop today.

CORNCOB VESSEL
Andean pottery was often made in the shape of the fruit and vegetables that were grown. Maize originated in Mesoamerica, but was widely grown in the Americas.

HOE
This tool was used as a spade to turn the soil of the plots.

Nazca pot showing a farmer, holding plants

TERRACES AT MACHU PICCHU
To get the highest yield from their crops, the Incas used sophisticated terracing and irrigation methods on hillsides in the highlands. Building terraces meant that they could use more land for cultivation, and also helped to resist erosion of the land by wind and rain.

TENDING CROPS
In the Andean region cultivating the soil was the basis of life. Farmers tended their crops using simple tools such as a digging stick, a clod breaker, and a hoe.

Hunting and fishing

HUNTING AND FISHING were important activities in Mesoamerica and in the Andean regions. Meat and fish were part of the diet, especially in the Andean region, depending on what was available in the area. Animal life in the Andes was most abundant in the high mountains of the north where large mammals such as vicunas (wild relatives of the llama) and deer roamed. In Mesoamerica, the largest creatures were the peccary (a relative of the pig) and the deer. These were hunted with bows and arrows. Smaller animals such as rabbits and dogs were caught in nets. Mesoamericans and South Americans fished for anything from shellfish to large fish and sea mammals with nets, harpoons, and by angling. They made hooks from sturdy cactus thorns, shell, and bone. Hooks were also made of copper in South America.

JADE FISH
People from coastal regions drew inspiration from fish and marine life to decorate pottery and jade objects.

IN THE NET
Catching waterfowl in nets was widespread in Mesoamerica around the lake areas.

Net tied to fisherman's back

GONE FISHING
This stirrup-spouted Moche vessel depicts a fisherman rowing on a balsawood raft. This was a typical scene on the Peruvian coast.

FAMILY TRADITION
Many trades, such as fishing, were passed from father to son. Boys were taught to fish at an early age, and at the age of 14 they went out fishing alone.

The Aztecs and the Mayas made their canoes from hollowed-out tree trunks

Raft made from woven reeds

REED RAFT
Watercraft were fashioned from reeds because of the shortage of wood in areas where little or no trees grew. This type of raft was – and still is – used high in the Andes around Lake Titicaca and on the coast. Large rafts between 4.5 and 6.1 m (14.5 and 20 ft) long were equipped with a wooden mast for raising and lowering the sail made of reeds.

FISHING NET
The lake system in and around Tenochtitlan provided people with fish and waterfowl, fresh water for drinking, and irrigation for crops. Sometimes fish were transported in canoes to markets and sold. Many nets in present-day Mexico are similar to those produced by the Aztecs and other Mesoamerican peoples. The most common net used by the Aztecs was bag-shaped like this one, made of fibre from the agave plant.

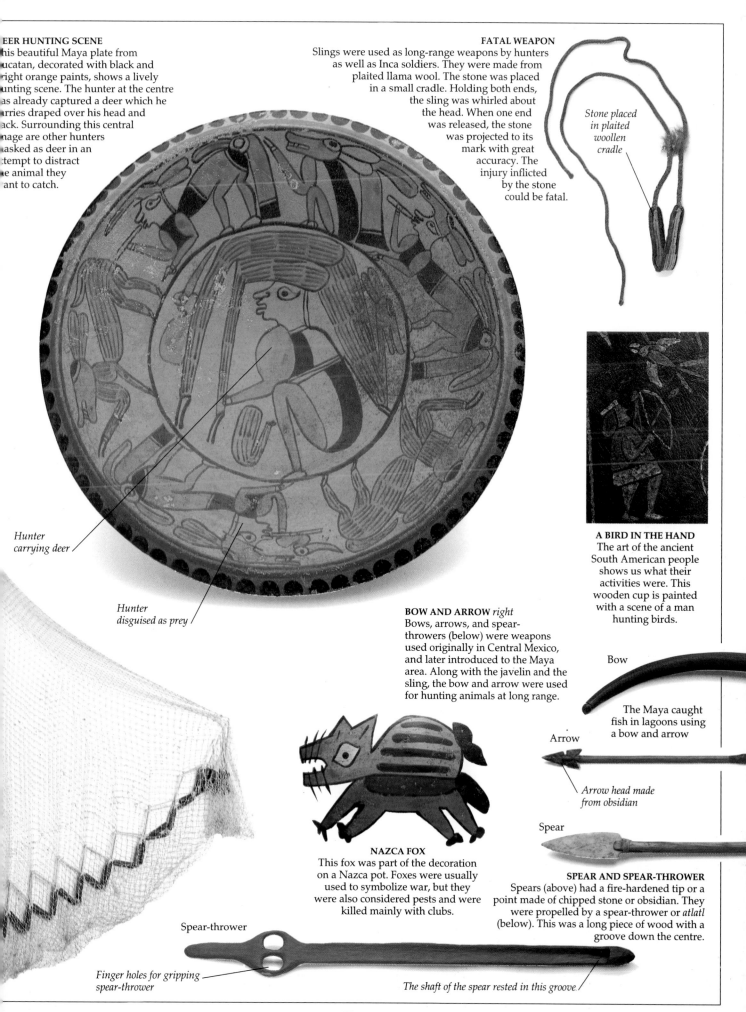

DEER HUNTING SCENE
This beautiful Maya plate from Yucatan, decorated with black and bright orange paints, shows a lively hunting scene. The hunter at the centre has already captured a deer which he carries draped over his head and back. Surrounding this central image are other hunters masked as deer in an attempt to distract the animal they want to catch.

Hunter carrying deer

Hunter disguised as prey

FATAL WEAPON
Slings were used as long-range weapons by hunters as well as Inca soldiers. They were made from plaited llama wool. The stone was placed in a small cradle. Holding both ends, the sling was whirled about the head. When one end was released, the stone was projected to its mark with great accuracy. The injury inflicted by the stone could be fatal.

Stone placed in plaited woollen cradle

A BIRD IN THE HAND
The art of the ancient South American people shows us what their activities were. This wooden cup is painted with a scene of a man hunting birds.

BOW AND ARROW *right*
Bows, arrows, and spear-throwers (below) were weapons used originally in Central Mexico, and later introduced to the Maya area. Along with the javelin and the sling, the bow and arrow were used for hunting animals at long range.

Bow

The Maya caught fish in lagoons using a bow and arrow

Arrow

Arrow head made from obsidian

Spear

NAZCA FOX
This fox was part of the decoration on a Nazca pot. Foxes were usually used to symbolize war, but they were also considered pests and were killed mainly with clubs.

SPEAR AND SPEAR-THROWER
Spears (above) had a fire-hardened tip or a point made of chipped stone or obsidian. They were propelled by a spear-thrower or *atlatl* (below). This was a long piece of wood with a groove down the centre.

Spear-thrower

Finger holes for gripping spear-thrower

The shaft of the spear rested in this groove.

Mesoamerican cities

THE PEOPLES OF MESOAMERICA built their cities in a variety of geographic and climatic areas. Some were built in the highlands and others in jungles or coastal regions. The Olmecs built their cities in tropical regions and the people of Teotihuacan, the Toltecs, and the Aztecs in the highlands. The Maya built their cities in both highland and lowland regions. These geographical differences influenced the architecture of the cities. As time passed the cities grew in size. The Olmecs (1200 B.C.) lived in small cities while Teotihuacan (A.D. 200) had an estimated 150,000 inhabitants or more. The central areas of Mesoamerican cities were reserved for religious and public buildings, and the houses of rulers and of the elite. The houses for the common people were built outside these areas.

CHICHEN ITZA
The Mayan city of Chichen Itza was built on a strategic position in the centre of the Yucatan Peninsula. It became an important commercial centre which kept contact with many areas. It is thought that Toltec invaders established themselves there.

Temple-pyramid *El Castillo* at Chichen Itza

TRIBUTE TOWNS
The Codex Mendoza (p. 7) gives the names of towns which paid tribute to Tenochtitlan, as well as the goods required. Each of these hieroglyphs (left) represents a subject town.

PALENQUE
This Mayan temple is situated in Palenque in the midst of tropical jungle. Hidden in the pyramid was the funeral chamber of lord Pacal (p. 53) who ruled for 68 years and was buried in his magnificent resting place in A.D. 683. His sarcophagus contained some of the most beautiful jade objects ever found in Mesoamerica.

Temple of the Inscriptions at Palenque

Shrine to Tlaloc, *god of rain*

Great temple of the Aztecs

Temple steps

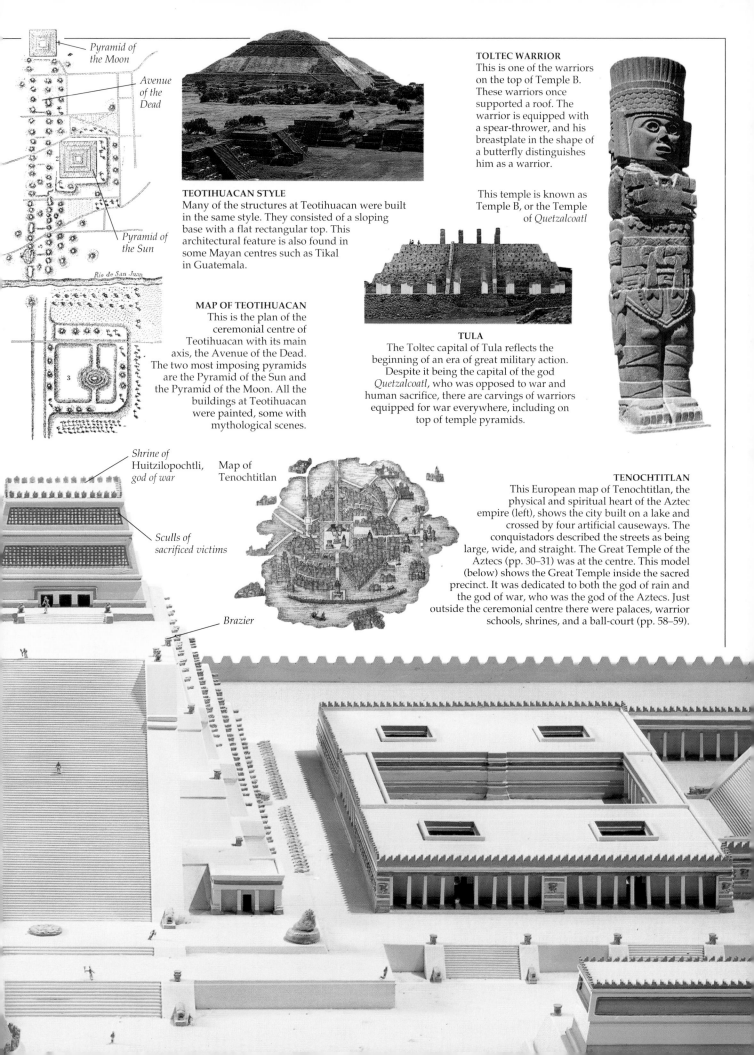

Pyramid of the Moon

Avenue of the Dead

Pyramid of the Sun

Rio de San Juan

TEOTIHUACAN STYLE
Many of the structures at Teotihuacan were built in the same style. They consisted of a sloping base with a flat rectangular top. This architectural feature is also found in some Mayan centres such as Tikal in Guatemala.

MAP OF TEOTIHUACAN
This is the plan of the ceremonial centre of Teotihuacan with its main axis, the Avenue of the Dead. The two most imposing pyramids are the Pyramid of the Sun and the Pyramid of the Moon. All the buildings at Teotihuacan were painted, some with mythological scenes.

TOLTEC WARRIOR
This is one of the warriors on the top of Temple B. These warriors once supported a roof. The warrior is equipped with a spear-thrower, and his breastplate in the shape of a butterfly distinguishes him as a warrior.

This temple is known as Temple B, or the Temple of *Quetzalcoatl*

TULA
The Toltec capital of Tula reflects the beginning of an era of great military action. Despite it being the capital of the god *Quetzalcoatl*, who was opposed to war and human sacrifice, there are carvings of warriors equipped for war everywhere, including on top of temple pyramids.

Shrine of Huitzilopochtli, god of war

Map of Tenochtitlan

Sculls of sacrificed victims

Brazier

TENOCHTITLAN
This European map of Tenochtitlan, the physical and spiritual heart of the Aztec empire (left), shows the city built on a lake and crossed by four artificial causeways. The conquistadors described the streets as being large, wide, and straight. The Great Temple of the Aztecs (pp. 30–31) was at the centre. This model (below) shows the Great Temple inside the sacred precinct. It was dedicated to both the god of rain and the god of war, who was the god of the Aztecs. Just outside the ceremonial centre there were palaces, warrior schools, shrines, and a ball-court (pp. 58–59).

Cities of the Andes

THE PEOPLE OF THE ANDEAN REGION lived either in highland or coastal areas. They built their cities to suit the location, from materials that were locally available. The typical highland building had a sloping thatched roof and masonry walls. On the coast, buildings tended to have mud-brick (adobe) walls with painted mud plaster, and flat roofs. Highland cities such as Machu Picchu could not be built on a regular grid plan, unlike the cities in flat coastal areas such as Chan Chan. The first buildings to be lived in as homes date back to the fourth century B.C. Public constructions such as government buildings, storehouses, bridges, and canals were built by taxpayers as a kind of labour tax, with the state providing the materials.

INCA STONEMASONS
The Incas are renowned for their fine stonework. Huge stone bricks were cut by masons using just a stone hammer and wet sand to polish them. The bricks fitted so closely that no mortar was needed.

OLLANTAYTAMBO
The Inca town of Ollantaytambo has some of the most impressive architectural remains in Peru. This doorway is built with rectangular blocks of stone. Each stone was precisely cut and fitted to a specific position.

TIAHUANACO
The city of Tiahuanaco (p. 10) is situated on a high plain nearly 4,000 m (13,100 ft) above sea level, rimmed by the mountains of the Andes. The stunning architecture of its ceremonial centre included an impressive number of stone sculptures. The Gateway of the Sun (above) was carved from a single block of stone. A carving above the doorway portrays a sun god.

Bird motif on adobe wall of compound, Chan Chan

Royal compound at Chan Chan, capital of the Chimu kingdom

ADOBE DECORATION
The Chimu decorated their thick adobe (mud) walls with moulded animals, usually associated with the sea – birds, fish, and men in boats.

CHAN CHAN
The Chimu people built proper urban centres, and Chan Chan, coastal capital of the Chimu empire, is a good example of this. The city was organized on a grid plan, and covered approximately 6 sq km (2.3 sq miles). It contained ten compounds, each enclosed by a high adobe (mud) wall. These are thought to be the royal residences and administrative centres of Chimu kings. Each king lived, died, and was buried in his secluded compound.

European map of Cuzco

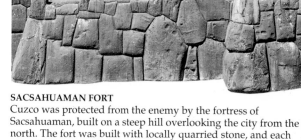
Stone walls of Sacsahuaman fort

CUZCO
The religious and political capital of the Incas is situated at the heart of the Andes with the mountains encircling it. The town was divided into sections by narrow paved streets, designed to represent the four quarters of the Inca empire. It had ceremonial plazas, palaces, and temples. Only the rulers and nobility lived in the city centre. This European drawing wrongly portrays Cuzco as a walled town. Much of Cuzco was destroyed by the Spanish, who built their city on Inca ruins.

SACSAHUAMAN FORT
Cuzco was protected from the enemy by the fortress of Sacsahuaman, built on a steep hill overlooking the city from the north. The fort was built with locally quarried stone, and each giant block was individually shaped. These three impressive stone walls – standing 16 m (52 ft) high – guarded the fortress.

INCA BATHS
Inca palaces sometimes had sunken stone baths for the kings to relax and bathe in. Water ran along stone channels into the bath. These baths at Tambo Machay, near Cuzco, were built at the site of a sacred spring. They were used by the Inca kings.

Machu Picchu

Inca baths at Tambomachay

MACHU PICCHU
Strategically positioned on the edge of the Inca empire, the remote city of Machu Picchu was probably built at the end of the 15th century. It was not discovered by the Spanish conquistadors, and was not rediscovered until 1911. The site is an outstanding example of Inca architecture – a natural fortress protected by steep slopes, surrounded by high mountain peaks, and approached from only one point. Of its 143 granite buildings, about 80 were houses, the rest being ceremonial buildings such as temples. Many mummies were found at Machu Picchu, most of them women.

COUPLE EMBRACING

In both Mesoamerica and the Andean region, a wife's role was to obey her husband. Even in art, women were often depicted in a passive position, and men in a more active position. This Mayan pottery statue shows a man embracing a woman. Both wear elaborate headdresses, earplugs, and necklaces which indicate that they were wealthy.

Figure has eyes and teeth inlaid with shell.

Family life

THE MESOAMERICAN MAN, as a husband and father, was responsible for the well-being of his household. He was expected to support his family, as well as his government, through hard work and by paying taxes. The woman, as a wife and mother, devoted her time and energy to running her household and caring for her children. Girls were taught domestic chores such as weaving and cooking, and sons followed their fathers while they worked. Children had free schooling, and nobles had their own schools. Family life was similar in the Andean region. The father worked to support the family and pay taxes; the mother worked in the home, helped her husband with his work, and cared for the children. Inca commoners had to educate their own children.

Aztec couple during marriage ceremony

JUST MARRIED

One of the rituals in an Aztec wedding ceremony was to tie the young man's cloak and the girl's blouse together. The wedding party followed, with dancing and singing.

FERTILE BLESSING

Both the Mesoamericans and the Incas considered it important for a married couple to have children. The Aztecs worshipped goddesses of fertility. This wooden Aztec sculpture is of a young woman dressed in a skirt and bare-breasted. She may be a goddess of fertility.

CELEBRATION

There were great celebrations when an Aztec baby was born. They lasted for days, during which astrologers checked to see when would be a favourable day for the baby to be named.

Stirrup handle

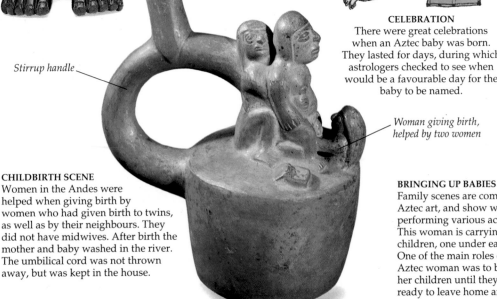

Woman giving birth, helped by two women

CHILDBIRTH SCENE

Women in the Andes were helped when giving birth by women who had given birth to twins, as well as by their neighbours. They did not have midwives. After birth the mother and baby washed in the river. The umbilical cord was not thrown away, but was kept in the house.

BRINGING UP BABIES

Family scenes are common in Aztec art, and show women performing various activities. This woman is carrying two children, one under each arm. One of the main roles of an Aztec woman was to bring up her children until they were ready to leave home and marry.

Steam made by throwing water on walls of bath-house

Fire for heating steam bath

STEAM BATHS
Bathing was a part of the daily family routine of the Aztecs, both for keeping clean and for purification. Almost every home had a steam bath alongside it. The bath-house was a small building that was heated by a fireplace. When water was thrown on the hot inside walls, the room filled with steam.

WOMAN CARRYING LOAD
The duties of women in the Andean region varied according to their rank. The woman depicted in this Moche vessel was probably a commoner's wife, and was expected to help her husband when necessary. This included carrying heavy loads on her back. She wears a strap that passes around her forehead to hold the load on her back.

Strap around forehead

PUNISHMENT
From the age of 11 years, disobedient Aztec children were punished in various ways by their parents. Punishments included pricking their skin with spines and making them inhale chilli smoke by holding them over a fire with chilli peppers.

CHILD'S PLAY
Until they reached an age where they had to help their parents with their work, young children played in and around the home. This pottery "toy" is in the form of a dog on wheels. "Toys" such as this one show that the Mesoamericans knew about the wheel. However, they used it for decorative purposes only, as they did not use the wheel for practical purposes such as on wagons to help them carry loads. "Toys" with wheels have been found mainly in graves in parts of the Gulf of Mexico. Toys in the form of dogs may have been thought to help the soul of the deceased to find his or her resting place in the afterlife.

Collar

Wheel turns on bolt

At home

Sharp wooden teeth

Maize cob used as cork

WATER GOURD
The gourd, a vegetable with a hard shell, was frequently used as a container after being dried out. Gourds were mainly used for carrying water. This type of gourd grows in most parts of the Americas.

THE AZTECS, MAYAS, AND INCAS lived in simple houses, many with only one main room and very little furniture. Inca houses were made of stone bricks or of mud (adobe), while most Aztec and Mayan houses were made of adobe. For the Aztecs, furniture was simply a few beds made of reed mats. There were also low tables, and reed chests for clothes. The Aztec home had an inside courtyard with a kitchen, and a small shrine to their gods. The bathroom was in a separate building. The homes of wealthy nobles and dignitaries had more rooms, more elaborate furniture, and a bigger garden.

INSIDE AN AZTEC HOUSE
An Aztec woman's home meant almost everything to her. She spent most of her day in the house, looking after the children, cooking, or weaving.

REED MAT
In Mesoamerica people sat, played, and slept on reed mats. This type of mat would have been used as a "rug" on the floor of most houses. It is thinner than the mats used as a "bed". Rich and poor had mats such as this one.

MULTIPURPOSE POT
This pot was used to store liquids and food. It was often kept upright with a ring made of reeds.

Bowl has three sturdy legs

TRIPOD BOWL
Potters working in Teotihuacan often made three-legged bowls like this, sometimes with a lid. Everyday pots were usually plain, but others had a pattern cut into the surface, or painted on like this one.

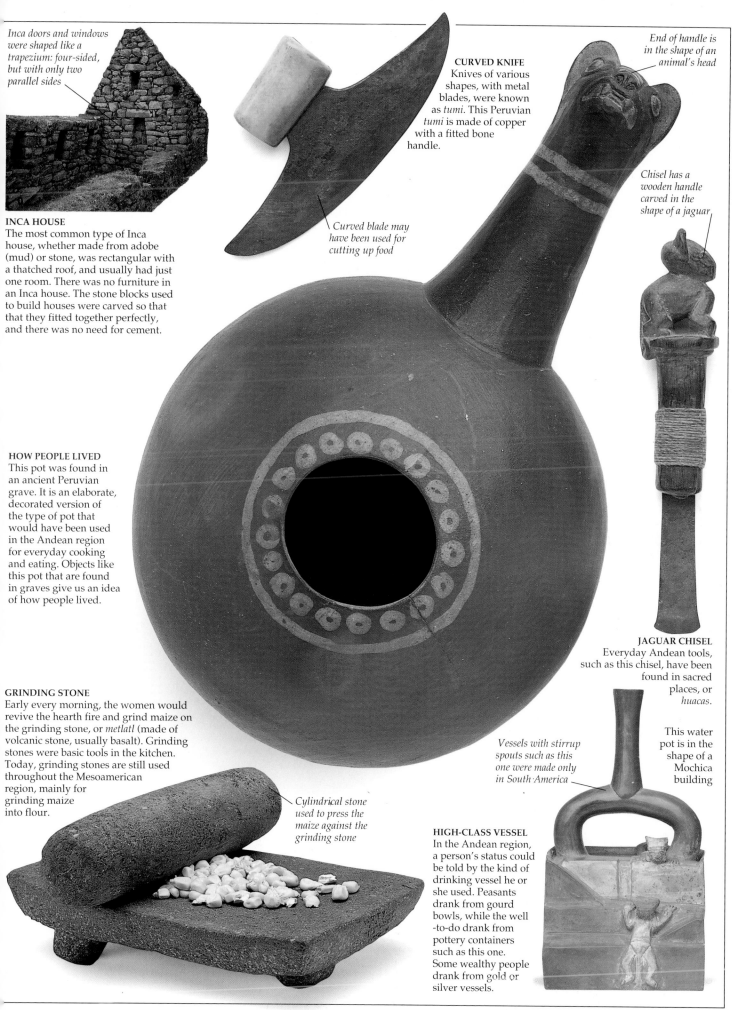

Inca doors and windows were shaped like a trapezium: four-sided, but with only two parallel sides

CURVED KNIFE
Knives of various shapes, with metal blades, were known as *tumi*. This Peruvian *tumi* is made of copper with a fitted bone handle.

End of handle is in the shape of an animal's head

Chisel has a wooden handle carved in the shape of a jaguar

Curved blade may have been used for cutting up food

INCA HOUSE
The most common type of Inca house, whether made from adobe (mud) or stone, was rectangular with a thatched roof, and usually had just one room. There was no furniture in an Inca house. The stone blocks used to build houses were carved so that that they fitted together perfectly, and there was no need for cement.

HOW PEOPLE LIVED
This pot was found in an ancient Peruvian grave. It is an elaborate, decorated version of the type of pot that would have been used in the Andean region for everyday cooking and eating. Objects like this pot that are found in graves give us an idea of how people lived.

JAGUAR CHISEL
Everyday Andean tools, such as this chisel, have been found in sacred places, or *huacas*.

This water pot is in the shape of a Mochica building

GRINDING STONE
Early every morning, the women would revive the hearth fire and grind maize on the grinding stone, or *metlatl* (made of volcanic stone, usually basalt). Grinding stones were basic tools in the kitchen. Today, grinding stones are still used throughout the Mesoamerican region, mainly for grinding maize into flour.

Cylindrical stone used to press the maize against the grinding stone

Vessels with stirrup spouts such as this one were made only in South America

HIGH-CLASS VESSEL
In the Andean region, a person's status could be told by the kind of drinking vessel he or she used. Peasants drank from gourd bowls, while the well -to-do drank from pottery containers such as this one. Some wealthy people drank from gold or silver vessels.

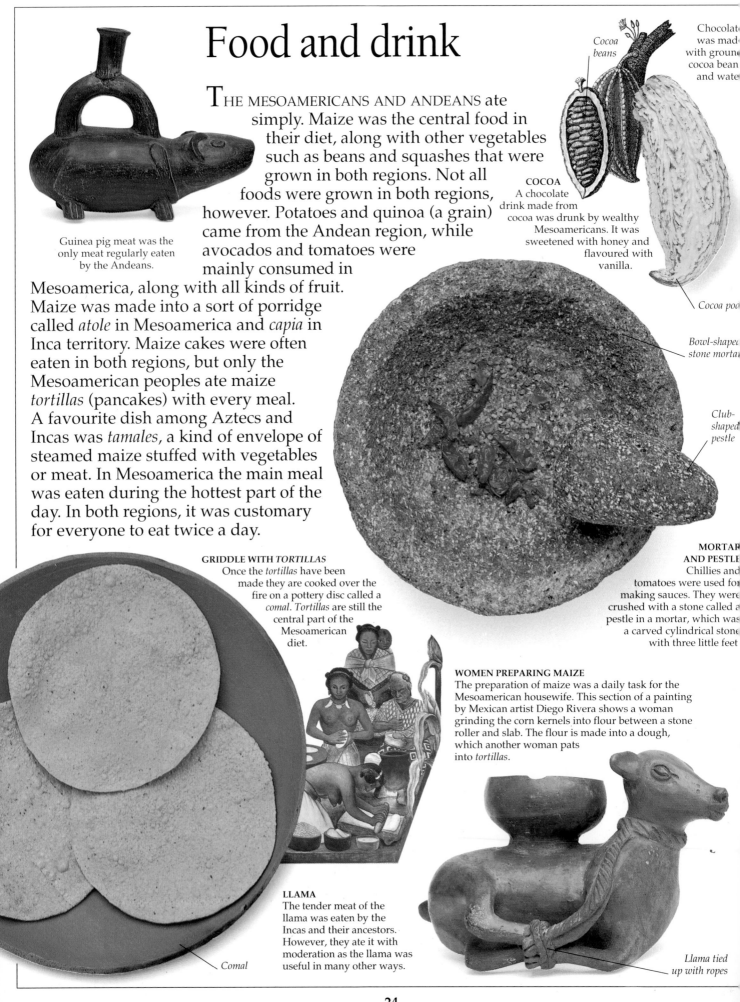

Food and drink

THE MESOAMERICANS AND ANDEANS ate simply. Maize was the central food in their diet, along with other vegetables such as beans and squashes that were grown in both regions. Not all foods were grown in both regions, however. Potatoes and quinoa (a grain) came from the Andean region, while avocados and tomatoes were mainly consumed in Mesoamerica, along with all kinds of fruit. Maize was made into a sort of porridge called *atole* in Mesoamerica and *capia* in Inca territory. Maize cakes were often eaten in both regions, but only the Mesoamerican peoples ate maize *tortillas* (pancakes) with every meal. A favourite dish among Aztecs and Incas was *tamales*, a kind of envelope of steamed maize stuffed with vegetables or meat. In Mesoamerica the main meal was eaten during the hottest part of the day. In both regions, it was customary for everyone to eat twice a day.

Guinea pig meat was the only meat regularly eaten by the Andeans.

Cocoa beans

Chocolate was made with ground cocoa beans and water

COCOA
A chocolate drink made from cocoa was drunk by wealthy Mesoamericans. It was sweetened with honey and flavoured with vanilla.

Cocoa pod

Bowl-shaped stone mortar

Club-shaped pestle

MORTAR AND PESTLE
Chillies and tomatoes were used for making sauces. They were crushed with a stone called a pestle in a mortar, which was a carved cylindrical stone with three little feet

GRIDDLE WITH *TORTILLAS*
Once the *tortillas* have been made they are cooked over the fire on a pottery disc called a *comal*. *Tortillas* are still the central part of the Mesoamerican diet.

WOMEN PREPARING MAIZE
The preparation of maize was a daily task for the Mesoamerican housewife. This section of a painting by Mexican artist Diego Rivera shows a woman grinding the corn kernels into flour between a stone roller and slab. The flour is made into a dough, which another woman pats into *tortillas*.

LLAMA
The tender meat of the llama was eaten by the Incas and their ancestors. However, they ate it with moderation as the llama was useful in many other ways.

Comal

Llama tied up with ropes

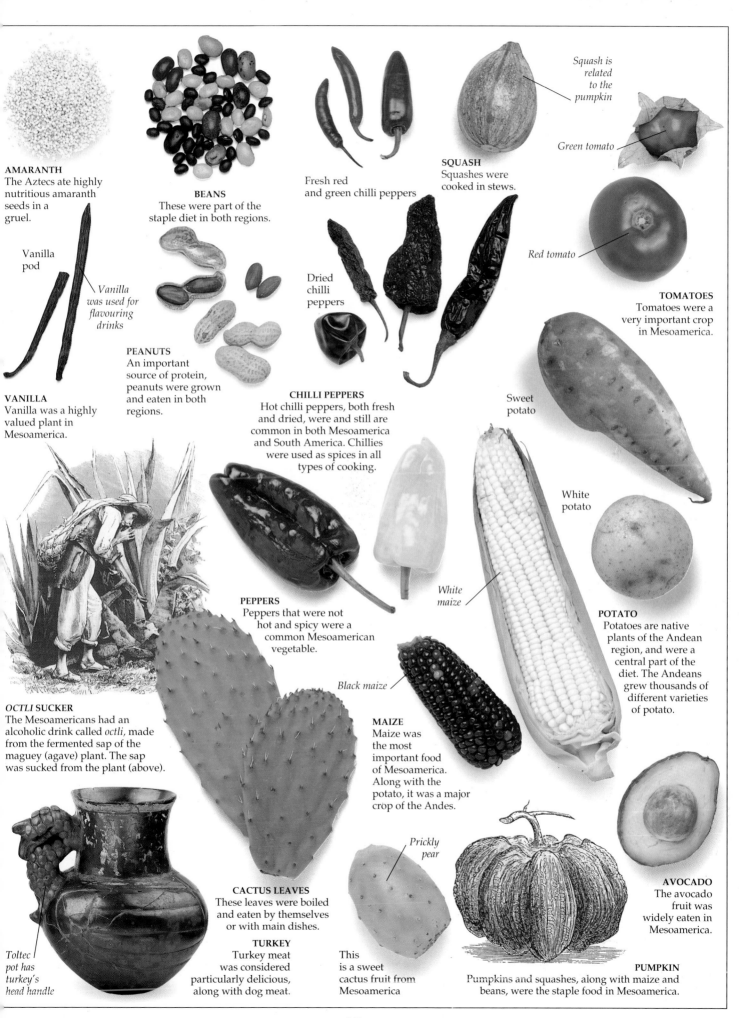

AMARANTH
The Aztecs ate highly nutritious amaranth seeds in a gruel.

Vanilla pod

Vanilla was used for flavouring drinks

VANILLA
Vanilla was a highly valued plant in Mesoamerica.

BEANS
These were part of the staple diet in both regions.

PEANUTS
An important source of protein, peanuts were grown and eaten in both regions.

Fresh red and green chilli peppers

Dried chilli peppers

CHILLI PEPPERS
Hot chilli peppers, both fresh and dried, were and still are common in both Mesoamerica and South America. Chillies were used as spices in all types of cooking.

Squash is related to the pumpkin

Green tomato

SQUASH
Squashes were cooked in stews.

Red tomato

TOMATOES
Tomatoes were a very important crop in Mesoamerica.

Sweet potato

White potato

POTATO
Potatoes are native plants of the Andean region, and were a central part of the diet. The Andeans grew thousands of different varieties of potato.

White maize

Black maize

MAIZE
Maize was the most important food of Mesoamerica. Along with the potato, it was a major crop of the Andes.

OCTLI **SUCKER**
The Mesoamericans had an alcoholic drink called *octli*, made from the fermented sap of the maguey (agave) plant. The sap was sucked from the plant (above).

PEPPERS
Peppers that were not hot and spicy were a common Mesoamerican vegetable.

Prickly pear

CACTUS LEAVES
These leaves were boiled and eaten by themselves or with main dishes.

TURKEY
Turkey meat was considered particularly delicious, along with dog meat.

This is a sweet cactus fruit from Mesoamerica

AVOCADO
The avocado fruit was widely eaten in Mesoamerica.

PUMPKIN
Pumpkins and squashes, along with maize and beans, were the staple food in Mesoamerica.

Toltec pot has turkey's head handle

Trade and tribute

IN MESOAMERICA and in the Andean region, it was the commoners who mainly supported the state by paying taxes. People of high rank did not pay taxes, nor did the sick and disabled, for example. In Inca territory, each province had to pay specific amounts of tribute to the government. At Tenochtitlan, the Aztec capital, the residents of each borough belonged to an institution called a *calpulli*, whose leader made sure that taxes were paid. Goods of all kinds were exchanged in both regions, and in Mesoamerica all the products of the land were sold in splendid marketplaces. Aztec merchants went on long expeditions to distant lands to trade for such items as tropical feathers, gold, fine stones, and jaguar skins.

RUNNER
This Moche pot depicts a runner. Runners, or *chasquis,* ran from one place to the next, usually carrying messages. The Incas had an excellent road system that was essential for controlling the empire, for trade, and for communication.

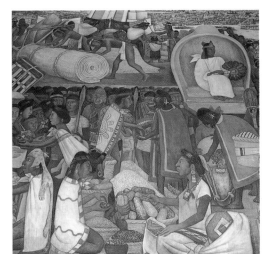

THE SALE OF MAIZE
Much can be learned from the murals of Diego Rivera about how the ancient Mexicans lived. Rivera, one of the most remarkable modern Mexican muralists, was well-read about life in Tenochtitlan. This detail of a busy market scene shows women selling various types of maize.

Jaguar headdress

WARRIOR'S SUIT AND SHIELD
Tunics and shields were very expensive items of tribute. Tunics were either made of feather-covered material or of animal pelts. The jaguar helmet (left) was the warrior's insignia as well as his protection. According to the Codex Mendoza, tribute of this kind had to be paid once a year.

Jaguar warrior's suit   Feather shield

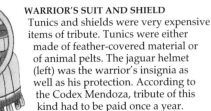

Ocelot skin

FUR TRADE
Animal skins were sold in the market at Tlatelolco. The skin of the puma was particularly valued by the Mayas, as its tawny colour reminded them of the sun. Jaguar skins were equally valued. The black spots were thought to symbolize the night sky. Jaguar skins were used as seats for the rulers, as book covers, and were also worn as cloaks.

Puma skin

Jaguar skin

TLATELOLCO MARKET
When the Spanish arrived in Mexico, they found that the market at Tlatelolco (the sister city of Tenochtitlan) was bigger and better stocked than any market in Spain. Supervisors regulated prices, and judges were present in case of disputes or theft. Much of the buying and selling was done by barter – exchanging products – although copper axes sometimes served as money in both Mesoamerica and in the Andes.

Inca treasurer records goods in storehouses on *quipu*.

Cocoa beans

Melon seeds

Axe heads

Quetzal feather

Jade beads

Tropical bird feather

TRADING
Items such as cocoa beans and feathers were in great demand, as vast quantities of each were paid in tribute. The merchants from Tenochtitlan and neighbouring major cities exported and traded luxury objects made from imported raw materials or materials obtained by tribute. In return for their goods they obtained goods such as tropical feathers (especially quetzal feathers), cocoa beans, animal skins, and gold.

INCA STOREHOUSES *left*
The Incas kept all kinds of supplies in storehouses used by government officials and those who were in need due to an illness, or after a crisis or a siege. They kept them full of items such as weapons, cloth, wool, potatoes, and maize.

Storing agricultural produce in government granaries

All the pottery stalls were placed together in the market

Simply decorated pottery vessel for everyday use

Simple pottery bowl

The market was a place where people exchanged news and goods

The warrior

WARFARE was a normal part of life in both Mesoamerica and the Inca region of South America, and city-states frequently fought each other. In Mesoamerica youths had to join the army at the age of 17 for a period of intensive training. The Inca and Mesoamerican peoples were educated in the arts of war, and the fighting spirit was encouraged. Among the Aztecs the best and most common way to climb the social ladder was by showing courage in battle. One of the main aims of going to war was to capture enemy warriors for sacrifice. Aztec warriors were in a constant "sacred war", as they believed that human sacrifice kept the sun in motion (pp. 36–37). Both the Incas and the Aztecs added newly conquered areas to their empires. As power and wealth grew, they developed a thirst for more conquests that would enrich the state and add to the glory of the emperor.

Slings like this Peruvian Chancay woven one, made from wool and cotton, were used in warfare. Warriors used stones as missiles.

TOLTEC WARRIOR
This sculpture shows a richly attired Toltec warrior wearing a feather headdress, earplugs, and a butterfly breastplate. In one hand he carries an *atlatl* or spear-thrower, and in the other a sheaf of darts.

CAPTURED
Aztec warriors who took captives were awarded costumes with distinctive designs, such as jaguar costumes and mantles. The more captives they took, the more elaborate the costume.

Club

AZTEC WEAPONS
A warrior usually carried spears of wood, with the blade edged with chert or obsidian, and a *maquahuitl* or war club made of wood which was about 76 cm (30 in) in length. It had grooved sides set with sharp obsidian blades. Warriors also carried stabbing javelins and round shields with protective feather fringes. Flint and obsidian knives such as these ones (left) were also used for human sacrifices.

Flint knife has a sharp serrated edge

Long, razor-sharp knife made from obsidian

OBSIDIAN WOODEN CLUB *below*
One of the main weapons used by the Aztecs was a *maquahuitl*, a wooden club edged with obsidian blades. Obsidian is a volcanic glass that is sharp enough to sever a horse's head.

EFFIGY POT
The Moche culture from the north coast of Peru often depicted warriors on pottery vessels, such as this warrior holding a club. Shields were often shown strapped to the wrists.

OBSIDIAN SPEAR *below*
A warrior usually carried one or two throwing spears of wood, the blades edged with flakes of sharp stone capable of inflicting deep cuts.

Obsidian blades around edge of spear

MOCTEZUMA'S STONE
This sculpted stone depicts the battles of the Aztec ruler Moctezuma I. The top of the stone was used for gladiatorial fights. It also served as a vessel for the hearts of sacrificial victims and other offerings. This detail (left) symbolizes the capture and incorporation of a city into the Aztec empire.

TERRACOTTA EAGLE WARRIOR
The most prestigious military orders were those of the eagle and the jaguar. Warriors wore either eagle or jaguar costumes. This life-size sculpture represents an eagle warrior. It is one of a pair that was found flanking a doorway to the chamber where the eagle warriors met, next to the Great Temple of the Aztecs in Tenochtitlan. The eagle was the symbol of the sun, to whom all sacrifices were offered.

Helmet shaped like an eagle's beak

The Aztec Warrior

The ideal Aztec warrior was noble, brave, and had to serve and respect the gods. Warriors were so important in Aztec Mexico that the Aztec ruler had to start his rule on the battlefield, adding cities and provinces to the empire, and capturing prisoners for ritual sacrifice, an essential part of the Aztec religion.

The eagle warrior's costume has wings on the arms, to imitate the eagle

Imitation talons

FEATHER SHIELD
All Aztec warriors carried a shield for protection. This one is made of jaguar skin and bright tropical feathers. Featherworkers were responsible for making shields, headdresses, fans, and other objects. Some of these were made of turkey and duck feathers, but many of the valuable objects were made of bright green quetzal feathers.

TEMPLE WARRIOR
This watercolour painting of a warrior figure decorated the doorway of a temple in the Mayan city Chichen Itza. The warrior is dressed and armed in a similar fashion to a Toltec warrior, as Toltec influence was great in some Mayan territories. He wears a shield around his waist, protective bands on one arm and on his legs, and is carrying spears.

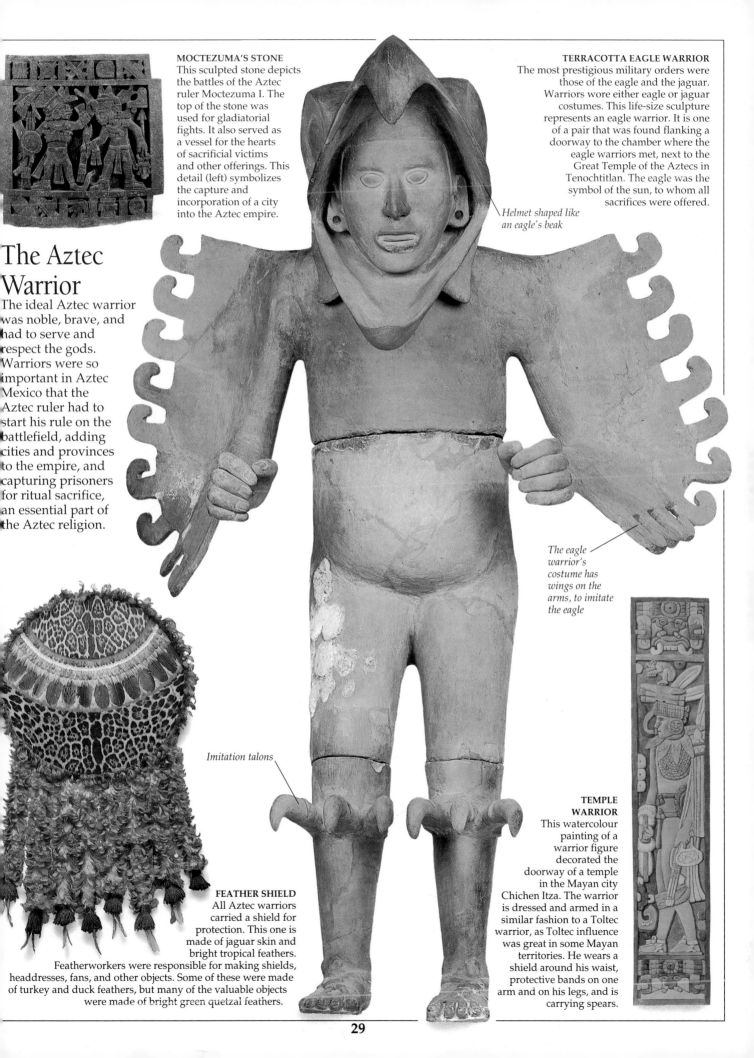

29

Religious life

RELIGION TOUCHED almost every aspect of Mesoamerican and Inca life. One of the many focal points for their religious rites were sacred buildings, or temples, dedicated to their gods. In the Andean region everyone worshipped a variety of shrines and objects and the natural forces associated with them, known as *huacas*. The Aztecs also worshipped sacred places. Within the official Inca state religion the sun was the most important god. It was a dominant force and a symbol of prestige and power. The Incas worshipped the sun mainly so that they would have abundant crops. The Aztec religion was also concerned with the sun. The Aztecs believed that they lived in the era of the fifth sun and that one day the world would end violently. In order to postpone their destruction, men performed human sacrifices. Their duty was to feed the gods with human blood, thereby keeping the sun alive.

Codex illustration of an Aztec temple at Tenochtitlan

TEMPLE OF THE GIANT JAGUAR
To worship their gods, the Mayas built magnificent ceremonial centres filled with temples, courts, and plazas. This majestic temple in Tikal stands in the middle of its ceremonial centre. It is a giant temple-pyramid with nine sloping terraces. The ornamental roof comb perched on the temple roof soars to a height of 65 m (212 ft).

Intihuatana *means "hitching post of the sun"*

STONE OF *INTIHUATANA*
The principal Inca temples for the cult of the sun were built by the government throughout the Inca empire. This stone in Machu Picchu worked as a solar clock and allowed people to calculate the winter solstice (21st of June) for the important festival of the sun god.

Priests performing rituals in temple during "new fire" ceremony

After sacrifice, bodies of sacrificial victims thrown down the stairs

AZTEC "NEW FIRE" CEREMONY
This religious event took place in temples every 52 years. When the day arrived, people extinguished all fires, and discarded idols and household utensils. The new century began when the sun's rays appeared again at dawn.

MODEL OF THE GREAT TEMPLE AT TENOCHTITLAN
At the heart of the city of Tenochtitlan was a walled precinct. Within it, sharing a single tall pyramid, were the twin shrines dedicated to *Tlaloc*, the god of rain and *Huitzilopochtli*, god of war and the tribal god of the Aztecs. The Great Temple was the physical and symbolic centre of the Aztec world, where human sacrifices and offerings to the Aztec gods took place. Each Aztec ruler tried to make a bigger and more impressive new temple. This model shows the many temples that were built, one above the other. The oldest, inner temple has a chacmool (a statue with a receptacle for hearts and blood) on the left and a sacrificial stone on the right. The excavators of the site found more than 6,000 objects buried as offerings to *Tlaloc* and *Huitzilopochtli*.

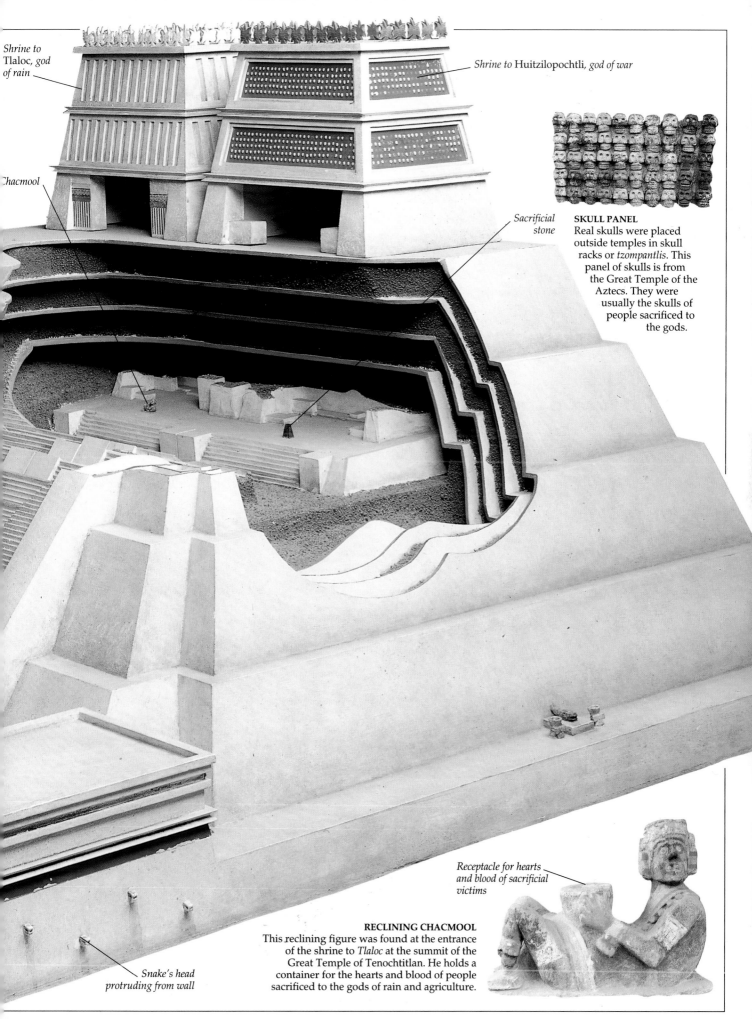

Shrine to Tlaloc, *god of rain*

Shrine to Huitzilopochtli, *god of war*

Chacmool

Sacrificial stone

SKULL PANEL
Real skulls were placed outside temples in skull racks or *tzompantlis*. This panel of skulls is from the Great Temple of the Aztecs. They were usually the skulls of people sacrificed to the gods.

Snake's head protruding from wall

Receptacle for hearts and blood of sacrificial victims

RECLINING CHACMOOL
This reclining figure was found at the entrance of the shrine to *Tlaloc* at the summit of the Great Temple of Tenochtitlan. He holds a container for the hearts and blood of people sacrificed to the gods of rain and agriculture.

Gods and goddesses

Aztec god from Codex Florentino

THE MESOAMERICAN and Inca people both worshipped many gods. They had similar religions – based on the worship of mainly agricultural gods – even though the gods' names and the symbols for them were different. People asked their gods for good crops and good health or for their welfare. The main Inca god was the creator god *Viracocha*. His assistants were the gods of the sun, moon, stars, and thunder, as well as the gods of the earth and the sea. As farming occupied such an important place in both regions, the "earth mother" or earth goddess was particularly important. The Aztecs adopted many gods from other civilizations. As with the Incas, each god was connected with some aspect of nature or natural force.

God of springtime, wearing the skin of a sacrificial victim

Xipe Totec god of springtime and of vegetation

RAIN GOD
Many Mesoamerican vessels and sculptures are associated with *Tlaloc*, the god of rain and agricultural fertility. It is likely that this water vessel depicts the face of the god of rain as it contains the vital liquid necessary to fertilize the earth.

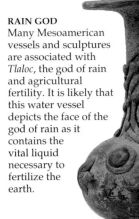

Tlaloc had "goggle eyes"

GOD OF THE SPRINGTIME
The Aztec god of the springtime and of vegetation was called *Xipe Totec* (our flayed Lord). He was also the patron of metal workers. The victims sacrificed in honour of this god were flayed (skinned alive). After flaying the victim, priests would wear the victim's skin. This symbolized the annual spring renewal of vegetation – in other words the renewal of the "earth's skin".

Feathered serpent, Quetzalcoatl

Rain god, Tlaloc

Reconstruction of temple of *Quetzalcoatl* in Teotihuacan

GOD OF NATURE
Quetzalcoatl, whose name means feathered serpent, was a god of nature – of the air, and of earth. The temple of *Quetzalcoatl* at Teotihuacan is decorated with large sculptures of feathered serpents, as this reconstruction shows.

Chicomecoatl wore a four-sided paper headdress with pleated rosettes at the corners

AZTEC MAIZE GODDESS
There were three goddesses associated with maize. This statue is of *Chicomecoatl*, the goddess of mature maize. This was the best seed corn of the harvest that was put away for sowing. There was also a goddess of tender maize, and one who was the personification of the maize plant.

Double maize cobs

WAR GOD
Huitzilopochtli (the Hummingbird of the left) was the tribal god of the Aztecs. In this illustration we see him armed with his serpent of fire and his shield.

GOD OF THE DEAD
Mictlantecuhtli was god of the dead in Aztec Mexico. Those who died a natural death went to the *Mictlan* where he lived, in the cold and infernal region of the fleshless.

The Inca people worshipped the moon and the sun

SEPTEMBER FESTIVAL
The Incas celebrated different religious festivities every month of the year. Here we see the celebrations for September dedicated to female goddesses. This festivity was celebrated under the protection of the moon and the sun gods.

WORSHIPPING THE SUN
The Incas worshipped the sun, *Inti*. Most agricultural religions often worshipped both the sun and the rain, as they are both essential for good harvests. The sun was the most important god of the Inca royal dynasty. Inca kings believed that they were descendants of *Inti*.

Gold disc

SKY OR MOON GOD
The handle of this Peruvian ceremonial knife is decorated with the image of either the sky or the moon god. His arms are opened wide, and he is holding two discs. He wears a beautiful filigree headdress with turquoise inlay.

Turquoise was used for the inlays of the eyes, necklace, earplugs and the clothing

Chac carries a bowl in his right and a ball of smoking incense in his left hand.

MAYA GOD OF RAIN
The Maya god of rain was called *Chac*. One of the sacrifices in honour of this god was to drown children in wells. In some Maya regions the god of rain was so important that the facades of buildings were covered with masks of *Chac*.

Life after death

Chancay "doll" found in grave

THE PEOPLE OF Mesoamerica and South America believed that after they died they would carry on living in another world. They were buried with goods of all descriptions that would be of use to them. By studying the goods found in graves, pre-Hispanic codices, and early colonial manuscripts, archaeologists have pieced together some of their beliefs about death and the afterlife. It was the way that Aztecs died, rather than the way they lived, that decided what would happen to them in the afterlife. If a person died a normal death, his or her soul had to pass through the nine levels of the underworld before reaching *Mictlan*, the realm of the death god. Warriors who died in battle, and women who died in childbirth, however, joined the sun god in the sky.

ALL WRAPPED UP
Many mummy bundles such as this one have been discovered in the Andean region. The corpse was placed in a flexed position and bound with cord to help maintain the pose. It was then wrapped in textiles and seated upright. Goods were placed around the mummy in the grave

DOLL COMPANION
Colourful figures found in Chancay tombs, such as this one, are called "dolls" because it is believed that they were used in daily life. They were placed with the deceased to serve them in the afterlife.

MUMMY OF DEAD KING
In Andean society, mummies were looked after as if they were alive. The living often consulted their dead in important matters. At special festivals, the mummies of emperors were paraded in the streets.

Mayan burial urn

THE RICH AND THE POOR
The more goods that were placed in a grave, the better-off the individual was. Wooden figurines such as this one of a man have been found in many Andean tombs. But tombs filled with golden objects, and where the corpse has been more elaborately prepared, indicate that everyone was not equal.

MAYAN BURIAL
The Mayas usually buried their dead under house floors or in the ground. Sometimes, however, they cremated the remains or buried them in caves, underground tanks, or urns. The privileged classes were buried in very elaborate tombs. One common type of burial for children was to place the corpse in a large urn, covered by a tripod (three-legged) vessel or pot fragment.

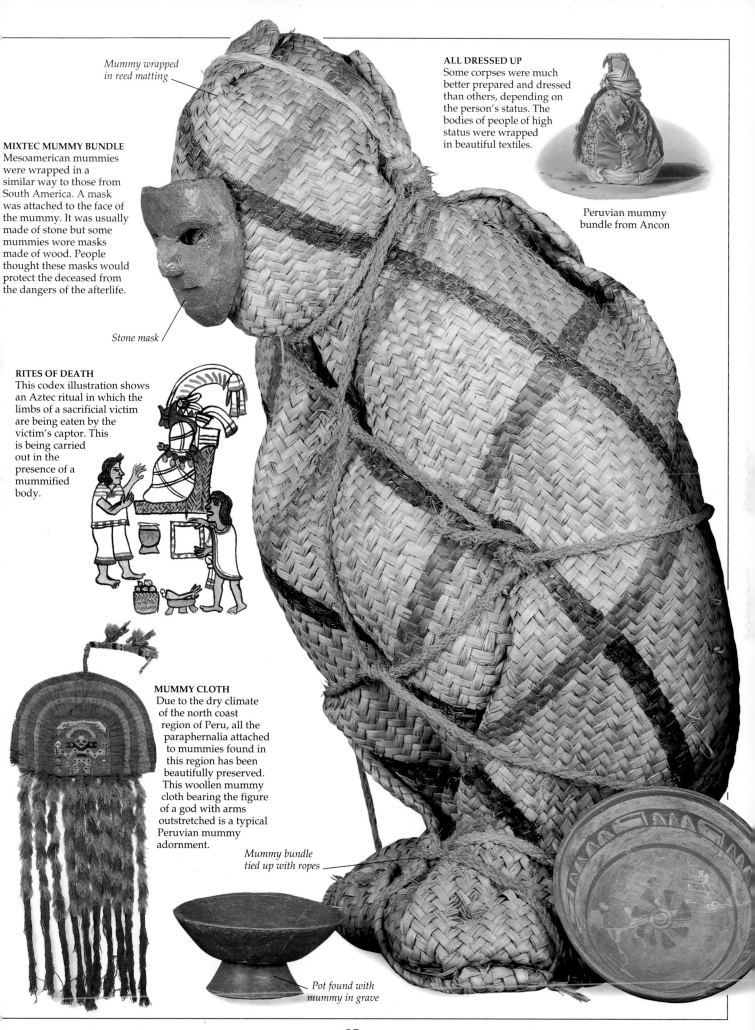

MIXTEC MUMMY BUNDLE
Mesoamerican mummies were wrapped in a similar way to those from South America. A mask was attached to the face of the mummy. It was usually made of stone but some mummies wore masks made of wood. People thought these masks would protect the deceased from the dangers of the afterlife.

Mummy wrapped in reed matting

Stone mask

ALL DRESSED UP
Some corpses were much better prepared and dressed than others, depending on the person's status. The bodies of people of high status were wrapped in beautiful textiles.

Peruvian mummy bundle from Ancon

RITES OF DEATH
This codex illustration shows an Aztec ritual in which the limbs of a sacrificial victim are being eaten by the victim's captor. This is being carried out in the presence of a mummified body.

MUMMY CLOTH
Due to the dry climate of the north coast region of Peru, all the paraphernalia attached to mummies found in this region has been beautifully preserved. This woollen mummy cloth bearing the figure of a god with arms outstretched is a typical Peruvian mummy adornment.

Mummy bundle tied up with ropes

Pot found with mummy in grave

Human sacrifice

Sacrifice was a religious ritual in Mesoamerica and in the Inca region of South America. The Incas and the Aztecs held special ceremonies that involved sacrifice in temples or on mountain tops, while the Mayas sometimes sacrificed victims in wells. Priests performed the sacrifices which took place at important festivals throughout the year. The Incas only practised human sacrifice in serious crises and for special events. For the Aztecs, sacrifice was more widespread and more frequent. The victims were men, women, and children – and sometimes animals. It was common for the Incas to ritually strangle women, while the Mayas sometimes drowned their victims and the Aztecs removed the victim's heart. Most sacrifices were performed in honour of the sun, rain, and earth gods. Human sacrifice was a communion with the gods: it was necessary to feed them to keep the cosmic order. People believed that just as the gods sacrificed themselves during the creation of the sun and the moon, they had to do the same.

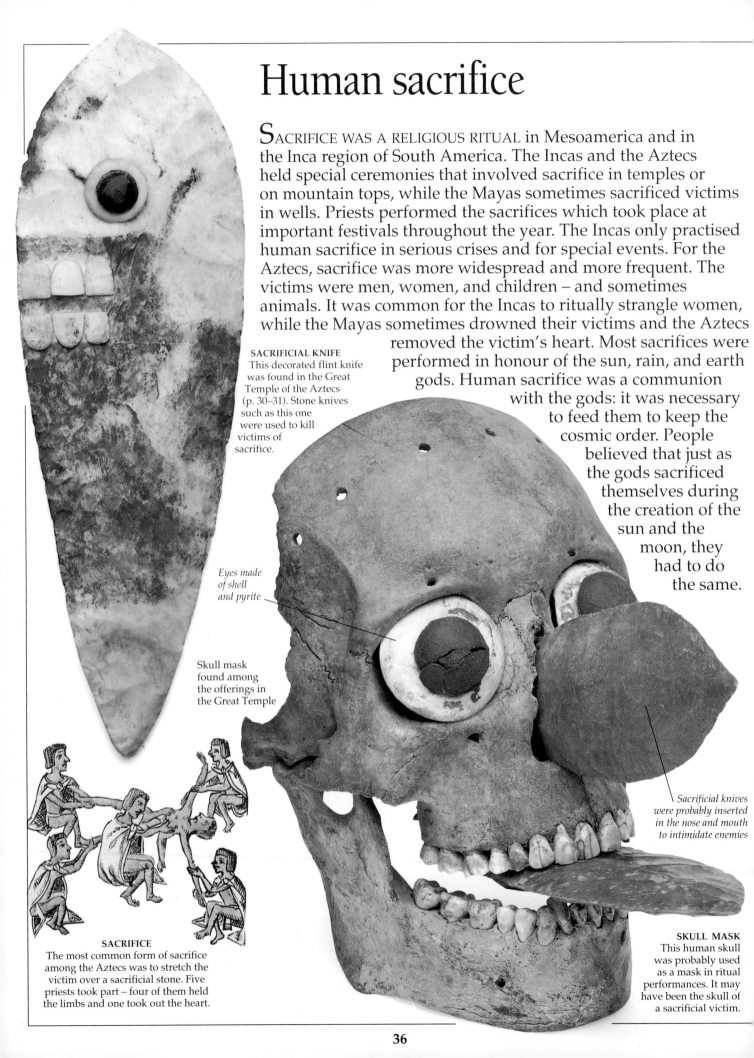

SACRIFICIAL KNIFE
This decorated flint knife was found in the Great Temple of the Aztecs (p. 30–31). Stone knives such as this one were used to kill victims of sacrifice.

Eyes made of shell and pyrite

Skull mask found among the offerings in the Great Temple

Sacrificial knives were probably inserted in the nose and mouth to intimidate enemies

SACRIFICE
The most common form of sacrifice among the Aztecs was to stretch the victim over a sacrificial stone. Five priests took part – four of them held the limbs and one took out the heart.

SKULL MASK
This human skull was probably used as a mask in ritual performances. It may have been the skull of a sacrificial victim.

AFTER SACRIFICE

Once an Aztec priest had taken the heart out, it was placed in a receptacle, such as the one below. The victim was then thrown down the temple stairs. The body was picked up and part of it, such as the thigh, was given as a reward to the victim's captor. The Aztecs practised cannibalism in some religious ceremonies under strict regulations. For example, enemy captives were ritually eaten, but only legs or arms could be consumed.

Illustration from Codex Magliabecchiano

The skull symbol often appears in Aztec art

SACRIFICIAL STONES AND VESSELS

This ritual vessel (right) may have been intended to contain the blood or the hearts of sacrificial victims. The outer surface is decorated with skulls. The skull was a symbol for fame, glory, or defeat depending on the situation. The stone below is one kind of stone that was used for the act of sacrifice. The victim would have been stretched over this stone while having their heart plucked out.

PRECIOUS HEART

This beautifully carved greenstone heart represents the most precious organ that the Aztecs could offer to their gods. Likewise, jade was considered the most valuable stone and the most precious material, far more so than gold. Jade was the symbol for life and agriculture.

MOUNTAIN TOP SACRIFICE

This ornate Moche water pot depicts men sitting high up in the mountain peaks. Mountain tops were sacred places. Here people worshipped the earth gods who were the providers of water and agriculture, and made human sacrifices to them. Water was considered to be the blood of agricultural life. Human sacrifices were performed for many reasons. They were generally considered a present to the gods in exchange for a favour requested – such as a good harvest. Those who were sacrificed were thought to be fortunate, since they were guaranteed a life of ease in the world to come.

High mountains and volcanoes were important places for sacred rituals

FLAYED ALIVE

This 19th-century illustration shows human sacrifice by flaying, or skinning a man alive. The ancient Peruvians performed this kind of ritual sacrifice. Skinning was also practised by the ancient Mexicans during agricultural festivities. Like the ancient Mexicans, the ancient Peruvians had many sacrificial victims dedicated to the sun *Inti* or to the creator god *Viracocha*.

Medicine

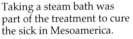

Bather resting in steam bath

Taking a steam bath was part of the treatment to cure the sick in Mesoamerica.

IN MESOAMERICA and in the Andean cultures, treatments for illnesses were a mixture of magic and a certain knowledge of the body. Mesoamerican midwives, healers, and physicians were often women who were well versed in the use of herbs. The Andeans believed that disease had a supernatural cause. They treated the sick with herbs for both magical and medicinal reasons. The Aztecs used certain minerals for medicine, as well as the flesh of some animals. The Incas used urine for treating fever, and often bled themselves. Inca surgeons bored holes in the skull and amputated limbs when necessary. Both Mesoamericans and Andeans used obsidian knives and lancets for surgery.

Snakeroot, taken for stomach pains

Pudding pipe-tree, a laxative, good for coughs and fever

MEDICINE SELECTION
Various plants and herbs were used as medicine. This root (left) was taken for rheumatism, and to treat bites of poisonous animals. Some roots were particularly useful for treating kidney complaints, and the round beans (below) were taken for circulation ailments. Quinine (from the bark of a Peruvian tree), despite its bitter taste, was taken to prevent and treat malaria.

Rabbit fern, good for treating rheumatism

Palm nuts, good for circulation

Quinine, taken for malaria

BANDAGING A LEG
Physicians had a good knowledge of the body and they were often right in their diagnosis. This Aztec surgeon is bandaging an injured leg.

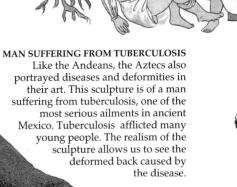

MAN SUFFERING FROM TUBERCULOSIS
Like the Andeans, the Aztecs also portrayed diseases and deformities in their art. This sculpture is of a man suffering from tuberculosis, one of the most serious ailments in ancient Mexico. Tuberculosis afflicted many young people. The realism of the sculpture allows us to see the deformed back caused by the disease.

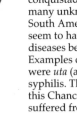

POT SHOWING MAN WITH SPOTS
Although the Spanish conquistadors brought many unknown diseases into South America, the Andeans seem to have known some serious diseases before their arrival. Examples of some diseases were *uta* (a kind of leprosy) and syphilis. The man portrayed on this Chancay vessel may have suffered from either disease.

Peyote

MARKET MEDICINE STALL
In Mesoamerica, wild plants and herbs were cultivated in botanical gardens for medicinal purposes and sold in markets. There were roots, seeds, maguey leaves, *copal* resin, and all kinds of plants for treating a range of ailments from snake bites to gout and fever. The ancient Mexicans believed that *copal* smoke cured diseases. Tobacco powder was inhaled by the Andeans to help clear the head, but in Mesoamerica it was also smoked for pleasure. Many seeds and roots were combined with vanilla, cocoa, and maize to make the medicine more palatable although many of these flavourings were considered medicinal in their own right.

CACTUS TOPS
Some plants and seeds, such as *ololiuhqui* seeds (Morning glory) were taken by the ancient Mexicans for medicinal purposes. These seeds as well as cactus tops or *peyote* (above) from northern Mexico were also widely taken as drugs. People who ate them experienced colourful hallucinations. Drugs causing hallucinations were also consumed in order for people to communicate with the gods.

Snakeskins and snake flesh were taken for various illnesses

Nuts and seeds

Leaves and roots

39

Writing and counting

Both the mesoamerican people and the ancient Peruvians kept records. However, what they recorded and how they did this was very different. Mesoamerican cultures had a picture-writing system and kept details of their history and administration, while the Peruvians had no written records. The Incas recorded information about tribute (p. 27) and goods in storage upon the *quipu*, an arrangement of knotted strings. Many Mesoamerican pictures (or glyphs) were pictograms, where an object was represented by a drawing. These glyphs also described ideas, for example a shield and a club signified war. This kind of writing has been kept in books (called codices), painted on walls and vases, and carved into objects ranging from stone monuments to tiny pieces of jade. The Mesoamericans were obsessed by counting, and the passage of time. Both the Aztecs and the Maya devised a *vigesimal* counting system based on the unit of 20, and had two calendars, the solar calendar and the sacred almanac.

ANCIENT AZTEC GODS
According to Aztec mythology the most ancient gods and the creators of the universe were "Lord and Lady of our sustenance". They are associated with time and the calendar.

Quipus were used to record the census and for taxation purposes

HIGH SOCIETY
Only the elite, a small fraction of Mesoamerican society, could read and interpret written records. This Maya woman is reading a book on her knee.

AZTEC DAYS OF THE MONTH
The Aztec solar calendar year was 365 days long. It consisted of 18 months of 20 days and five extra days that were thought to be unlucky. This illustration shows four days of the month – flint knife, rain, flower, and alligator.

MAYA PAINTED BOOK
There are four Maya codices in existence. This one, the Codex Tro-Cortesianus, contains information about divination (predicting the future) and rituals for Maya priests. Codices were made of carefully prepared paper, cloth made from fibres of the maguey plant, or animal skin. The Maya codices were written or painted with fine brushes on long strips of bark paper, folded like screens and covered with a layer of chalky paste (gesso).

Numbers recorded with knots of varying sizes

Facsimile copy of original Codex Tro-Cortesianus

INCA ACCOUNTANT
A special accountant was in charge of keeping records. He was skilled in recording figures, whether of people, llamas or what tribute was to be paid.

INCA COUNTING DEVICE
The *quipu* was a length of cord held horizontally, from which knotted strings of various thicknesses and colours hung vertically. The information recorded varied according to the types of knots, the length of the cord, and the colour and position of the strings.

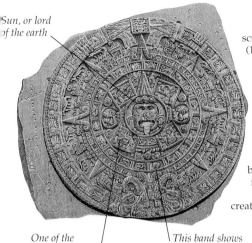

Sun, or lord of the earth

One of the previous four world creations

This band shows the 20 days of the month

AZTEC SUN STONE

This stone is the largest Aztec sculpture ever found, measuring 4 m (13.2 ft) in diameter. At the centre of the stone is the face of the sun, or that of the lord of the earth. This carving is sometimes called the "Calendar Stone". In fact, it represents the Aztec belief that the universe had passed through four world creations which had been destroyed. We are now in the fifth, doomed to be destroyed by earthquakes. According to Aztec mythology, the sun, the moon, and human beings were successfully created at the beginning of the fifth era.

The date glyph on this sculpture is "day one death"

RIDDLE OF THE GLYPHS

The study of Maya hieroglyphic writing started in 1827. By 1950, names of gods and animals had been identified. In 1960, researchers realized that Maya inscriptions were primarily historical. They deal with the births, accessions, wars, deaths, and marriages of Maya kings. This Maya stone carving was placed over doors and windows. It has a glyph that dates it to the sixth century.

BUNDLE OF YEARS

The Aztecs divided time into "centuries" of 52 years. At the end of each cycle and the beginning of a new one an Aztec ceremony called "the binding of the years" took place. In sculpture each cycle is represented by a bundle of "reeds" accompanied by dates. This sculpted stone bundle symbolizes the death of an Aztec century.

Bars and dots are Mayan glyphs for numbers

This codex was read from top to bottom, and from left to right

Glyphs showing five gods

Glyphs painted onto fine layer of gesso

Weaving and spinning

Nazca textile with fringed border

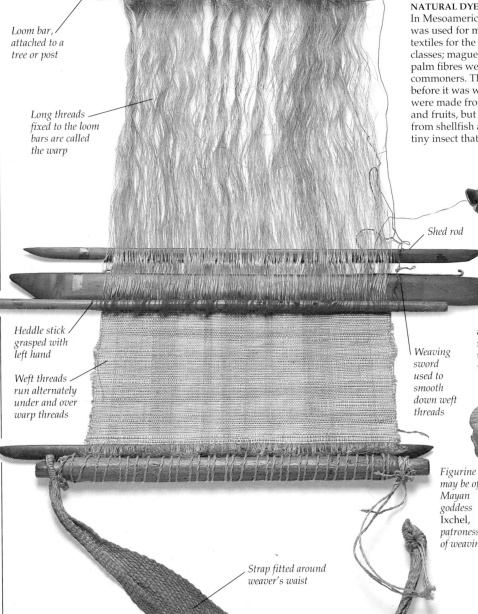
Much of the sophisticated Andean weaving was made on the back-strap loom

NO OTHER PEOPLE in the Americas have left such a wealth of marvellous woven textiles as the ancient Peruvians have. Their exquisitely worked textiles have survived in graves in areas of Peru that have a desert-like climate. The tradition of weaving and spinning was practised by all women, both in Mesoamerica and in the Andean region. They were expected to spin and weave for their families' needs, as well as contributing woven goods for payment of tribute and taxes to their rulers. Textiles were woven mainly from cotton and maguey fibre in Mesoamerica, while alpaca and llama wool were widely used in the Andean region.

Loom bar, attached to a tree or post

Long threads fixed to the loom bars are called the warp

NATURAL DYES
In Mesoamerica, cotton was used for making textiles for the upper classes; maguey, yucca, and palm fibres were woven for the commoners. The yarn was dyed before it was woven. Some dyes were made from the juice of flowers and fruits, but dyes were also extracted from shellfish and from the cochineal, a tiny insect that lives on the cactus plant.

Shed rod

BACK-STRAP LOOM
The most common loom used throughout the Americas was the back-strap loom (left). It is still widely used today. The loom consists of two loom bars, poles holding the warp, that are hooked to a support at one end, and pulled taut by a belt around the weaver's back at the other end. The weft (horizontal) thread is passed under and over the strands of the warp (vertical) threads using a heddle stick and a shed rod to lift up alternate strands. To alter the pattern or introduce more colour, more heddles are used, or different groups of warp threads are lifted up.

Heddle stick grasped with left hand

Weft threads run alternately under and over warp threads

Weaving sword used to smooth down weft threads

Figurine may be of Mayan goddess Ixchel, patroness of weaving

Strap fitted around weaver's waist

MAYA LADY WEAVING
This Maya figurine shows a young lady sitting on the ground, weaving with a back-strap loom.

DECORATED BORDER
The majority of ancient Peruvian textiles were decorated with motifs which varied from abstract geometric shapes – squares, oblongs, and frets – to stylized images of birds, fish, animals, and human beings.

Inca woman spinning and twisting as she walks

SPIN AS YOU WALK
The fine quality of woven fabrics depended on the quality of the yarn and how finely it was spun.

EMBROIDERED TEXTILE
The ancient Peruvians were also skilled embroiderers. They created fantastic images with just a few stitches. This Inca woven textile has an embroidered design of stylized heads and serpents, perhaps symbolizing thunder.

Bamboo needle case

NEEDLECASE
Needles were useful weaving tools, and were kept safely in cases such as this one. Needles were used for sewing and darning as well as for weaving with. They were made of cactus spines and of copper.

Needles made of cactus spines

Wooden whorl

Decorated weaving tool found in work-basket

NAZCA WEAVER
The Nazca culture is renowned for its beautiful textiles. They decorated their pottery with designs that they also used in their weavings. This pot shows a woman holding a spindle in one hand.

Spindle and whorl

HOW TO SPIN
With the spindle upright, the spindle and whorl are spun between the fingers. This teases out the yarn, which is then twisted into a fine thread and wound around the spindle.

Ball of unspun cotton

Spindle with spun cotton yarn wound around it

REED WORK-BASKET
This Peruvian reed work-basket contains balls of yarn, spindles, and raw cotton. Reed work-baskets were often buried with their owners so that females could continue weaving in the afterlife. Most weaving probably took place in the outer courtyards of dwellings. Women and men were required to weave, spin, and produce cloth and cord for the empire as a form of taxation. Weaving was done by women while men made cordage and cloth.

Skein of dyed cotton thread

Women kept their sewing and weaving tools in baskets like this one

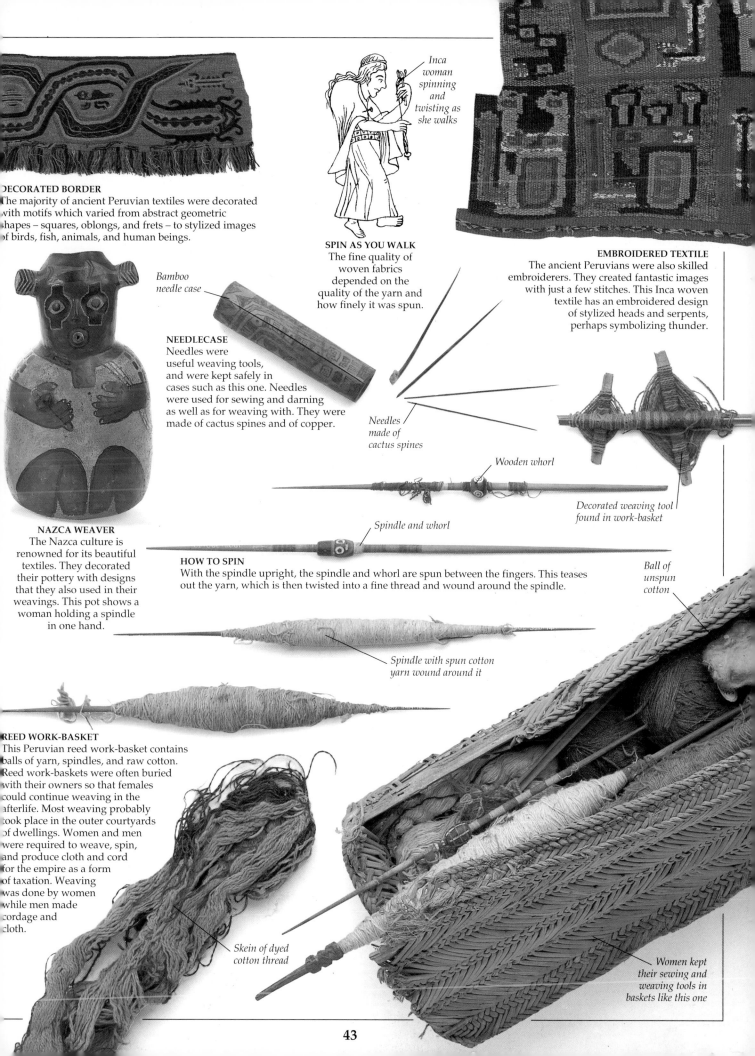

Clothes and accessories

CLOTHING styles were very different in Mesoamerica and South America, but in both regions they reflected a person's social class. People who wore clothes of fine material with colourful and elaborate decoration were of high status. The Incas made their clothes from wool, although on the coast cotton was preferred. Alpaca wool was worn by ordinary people and silky vicuna wool by the nobles. In Mesoamerica, garments were made from cotton or other plant fibres. All items of clothing were very simple. Many were just a piece of material draped around a part of the body. Men from both regions wore loincloths. Aztec women wore a skirt wrapped around the hips. Men wore cloaks draped over the shoulder. Some items of clothing – ponchos and tunics – slipped over the head and were sewn at the sides.

CAPPING IT ALL
In the Andean region people wore knitted wool or cotton caps. This handsome Chimu cap with colourful panels is unusual because it is made from woven wool.

SANDAL
The Incas made sandals with leather from the neck of the llama. In other regions sandals were made of wool or, as in this case, the fibre of the aloe plant.

Plaited wool fastening

IN THE BAG
All Peruvian men carried a small bag under their cloak, slung over the shoulder. In it they carried coca leaves for chewing, and amulets (good-luck charms).

SLEEVELESS PONCHO *right*
Some ponchos were decorated with fine patterns. They were such important garments that the dead were buried with ponchos. In the highland regions of Peru, both men and women wear ponchos to the present day.

Woven headband

ANDEAN WOMAN'S DRESS
Although this is an 18th-century impression of a Peruvian woman, her clothing is similar to that worn by an Inca woman: a long dress of woven rectangular cloth, with a long cloak and sandals.

CHILD'S PONCHO *left*
Finely woven ponchos covering mummies have been discovered in some ancient Peruvian graves. This small poncho was discovered in a child's grave. It is woven from wool, with a design of birds in diagonal bands.

SHELL NECKLACE
In Mesoamerica, only the ruler and nobles could wear jewellery such as headbands, armbands, or nose, lip, and earplugs. Even necklaces made of shells like this one could not be worn by everyone.

DIFFERENT CLOTHES, DIFFERENT JOBS
Aztec people wore clothes that suited their role in society. The lavish headdresses and rich materials worn here show that these are people of high rank.

COORDINATED CLOTHES
This Mayan woman is wearing a matching turban, skirt, and shawl. Her beautiful long hair is tied back with white ribbons. She wears a feather ornament in one ear and a bracelet probably made of leather.

Parasol

Elaborate headdress with two folds

SOPHISTICATED LADY
This richly attired figure is obviously a high-ranking Mayan woman. She wears a headdress with two folds, and blue earplugs which perhaps represent turquoise. Her beaded necklace is similar in shape to Mayan jade necklaces and she wears bracelets on both arms. With one hand she protects her face with a parasol.

FANCY CAPE
Capes like this one were worn throughout Mesoamerica. This army commander is of high rank, so his cape is finely decorated.

Robe with holes for arms and square-cut neck

MALE FASHION
This life-size head of a Mixtec man shows what adornments they wore. He has a headband tied around his forehead, with a bird's head at the centre, and blue discs at the sides. His hair is loose, and he wears round blue earplugs. His mouth is painted with black and white spots, resembling a mouth ornament.

Mayan women often walked barefoot

Master potters

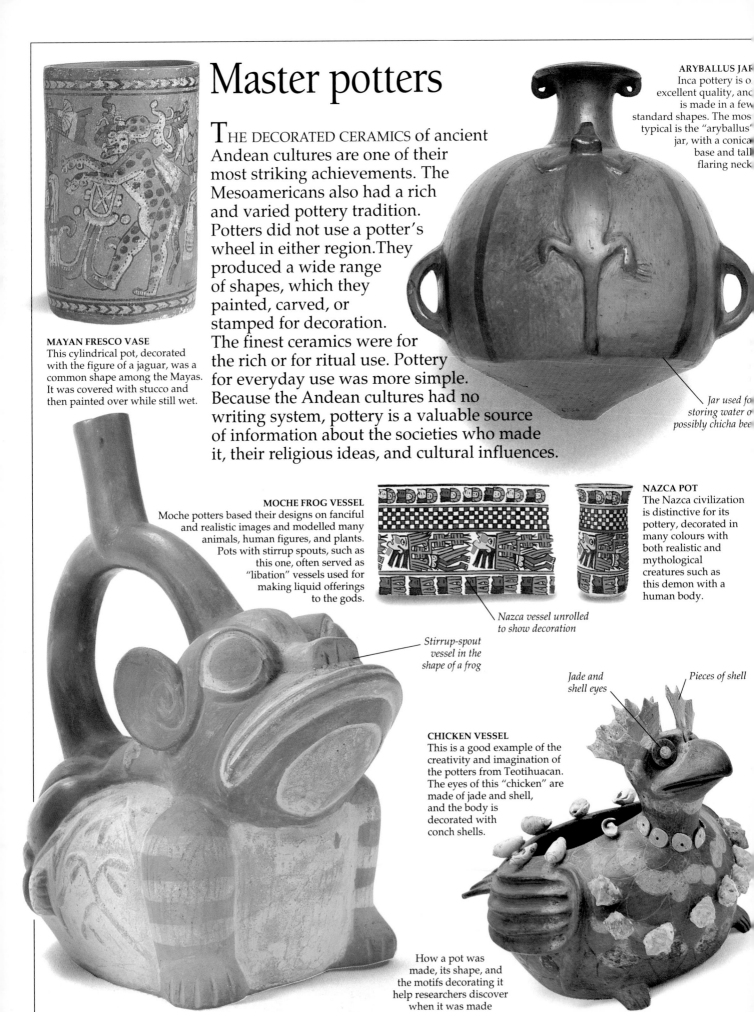

THE DECORATED CERAMICS of ancient Andean cultures are one of their most striking achievements. The Mesoamericans also had a rich and varied pottery tradition. Potters did not use a potter's wheel in either region. They produced a wide range of shapes, which they painted, carved, or stamped for decoration. The finest ceramics were for the rich or for ritual use. Pottery for everyday use was more simple. Because the Andean cultures had no writing system, pottery is a valuable source of information about the societies who made it, their religious ideas, and cultural influences.

MAYAN FRESCO VASE
This cylindrical pot, decorated with the figure of a jaguar, was a common shape among the Mayas. It was covered with stucco and then painted over while still wet.

ARYBALLUS JAR
Inca pottery is o excellent quality, and is made in a few standard shapes. The mos typical is the "aryballus" jar, with a conica base and tall flaring neck

Jar used fo storing water o possibly chicha bee

MOCHE FROG VESSEL
Moche potters based their designs on fanciful and realistic images and modelled many animals, human figures, and plants. Pots with stirrup spouts, such as this one, often served as "libation" vessels used for making liquid offerings to the gods.

Stirrup-spout vessel in the shape of a frog

Nazca vessel unrolled to show decoration

NAZCA POT
The Nazca civilization is distinctive for its pottery, decorated in many colours with both realistic and mythological creatures such as this demon with a human body.

Jade and shell eyes

Pieces of shell

CHICKEN VESSEL
This is a good example of the creativity and imagination of the potters from Teotihuacan. The eyes of this "chicken" are made of jade and shell, and the body is decorated with conch shells.

How a pot was made, its shape, and the motifs decorating it help researchers discover when it was made

PAINTING PALETTE
It is very likely that the Teotihuacan potters used some kind of palette to mix pigments. They used both vegetable and mineral colours. This pottery object may have been used as a palette for the pigments.

FIGURINE AND MOULD
This figurine of a goddess with two children was modelled using a clay mould. It may have been placed on the altar in a peasant house as they could not afford anything bigger or of better material.

Clay goddess   Mould for goddess

Aztec potters usually decorated the inside of bowls

AZTEC BOWL
The decoration on this bowl is based on an abstract pattern of zig-zag lines. Painted decoration was usually only in two colours, like on this bowl.

Hummingbird perched on rim

This urn contained human ashes

MIXTEC CUP
This beautiful Mixtec cup is decorated with a hummingbird perched on the rim. The base has the characteristic "step fret" motif often used by Mixtec artists.

Urn found at the Great Temple of the Aztecs

"Step fret" motif

FUNERARY URN
Some pottery vessels were not painted, but rather the decoration was cut into the surface. The picture on one side of this urn is of a bearded god wearing a necklace. He holds a spear-thrower in one hand, and spears in the other.

Featherwork

THE BRIGHT COLOURS and natural sheen of tropical bird feathers made them a valuable item for trade and tribute in Mesoamerica and in the Andean region of South America. Tropical birds were hunted and raised in captivity for their feathers, which were worked into stunning patterns and designs. For the Mesoamericans, the iridescent green feathers of the quetzal were the most prized. The Incas used feathers as part of their dress, and wove them into clothing for special occasions. They also used them to decorate headdresses and tunics, and to make mosaics (a design of feathers glued to a backing to decorate hard items such as shields). Skilled Aztec feather workers made beautiful garments only for the nobility, while the Mayas made superb items such as headdresses that were extended at the back and made the wearer look like a bird that had just landed.

FEATHER MOSAICS
Ancient Mexico had a guild of expert feather workers who used intricate methods of gluing and weaving feather mosaics. These methods were studied and illustrated by a Spanish friar called Bernardino de Sahagún.

FEATHER SHIRT AND HEADDRESS
This type of feather shirt is known as a *poncho*. Each of the feathers has been carefully stitched to a cotton cloth to make up the design of stylized owls and fish. Several Peruvian cultures, such as the Chimu and the Inca, had expert featherworkers.

Tall feather headdress

Fan made of macaw feathers

Holder made of plaited brown wool

WAVE OF COLOUR
The ancient Peruvians made very colourful fans using feathers from tropical birds. These fans were useful for keeping cool in hot climates. The Peruvians made many practical objects with feathers, especially from parrots and macaws as these were their favourite birds.

FEATHER HEADDRESS
This simple Peruvian headdress was possibly made from
feathers taken from birds in the Amazon region. Items made
from the feathers of exotic birds were status symbols.

trings were used
o tie the headdress
round the head

MOCTEZUMA'S HEADDRESS
This is a replica of a headdress said to have
belonged to Moctezuma, the last Aztec
ruler. The headdress was part of the booty
sent by Cortés to Spain (pp. 62–63). It is
made of green quetzal feathers,
blue cotinga feathers,
and gold
discs.

*Headdress
contains the
feathers of at
least 250 birds*

*Fan has a
butterfly on
this side and
a flower on
the other*

MEXICAN FAN
This fan was
made with the
feathers of several
kinds of bird.
Sumptuous fans such as this
one were used by dignitaries.

Bamboo handle

*Feather
headdress*

k of
w and
n feathers

Rear
view

Front
view

Side
view

WARRIOR OUTFIT
An Aztec warrior's
rank was reflected
in the kind of
feather suit he
wore. This
elaborate
feather suit,
complete with
shield and
headdress, was
worn by a
high-ranking
warrior.

*Feather
headdress*

Feather suit
belonging to
a warrior of
high status

*Feather
shield*

FEATHERS IN STONE
This carved stone Atlantean figure
from a temple at Chichen Itza was
originally painted all over. The
watercolours show two views of it
s it would have been. The figure
s dressed in a full-length feather
loak and a feather headdress.

REBUILDING THE PAST
Watercolours like this
one by British artist Adela
Breton give us an idea of
how pre-Columbian sculptures
were painted, and what the
buildings at Chichen Itza
looked like originally.

*Feather
suit*

Precious metals

THE PERUVIAN TRADITION of crafting magnificent artefacts from precious metals began 3,500 years ago, the age of the oldest piece of precious metalwork found in the Andes. Methods of metalworking gradually developed, and metals were widely worked in South America before the Christian era. They were introduced to Mesoamerica in about 850 B.C. Some of the most common precious metals in the Americas are gold, silver, and platinum. These were mostly used for making objects for ritual use, trinkets, and jewellery. Combinations of gold and silver, and copper and gold (called *tumbaga*) were also used Because of the value attached to gold, wearing gold jewellery was a sign of a person's wealth and power. When a wealthy person died, his or her tomb would be filled with precious gold and silver objects, encrusted with precious stones.

LIP ORNAMENT
Eagle heads like this one made by the Mixtecs were popular as decoration for lip plugs, or labrets. The Mixtecs produced most of the gold work for the Aztec elite. Labrets were inserted through a hole made below the bottom lip.

GOLD CREATURE
The ancient South American goldsmiths produced many and fantastic creatures. This figure is a mixture of human and animal forms.

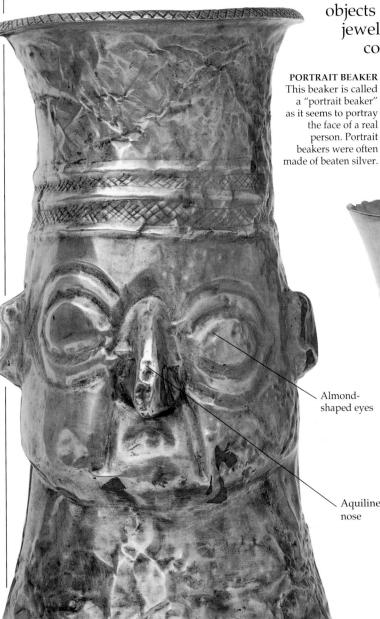

PORTRAIT BEAKER
This beaker is called a "portrait beaker" as it seems to portray the face of a real person. Portrait beakers were often made of beaten silver.

Almond-shaped eyes

Aquiline nose

Beaker has hammered bird design

SILVER BEAKER
These beakers are usuall known as *keros*. Many of them have been found throughout the Andean region placed in cemeterie together with other object near the corpses. Some *ker* were used to drink *chicha*, kind of beer made of maiz Some beakers were inlaid with turquoise. This beake is the work of a Chimu metalsmith, showing it wa made before the Inca peric

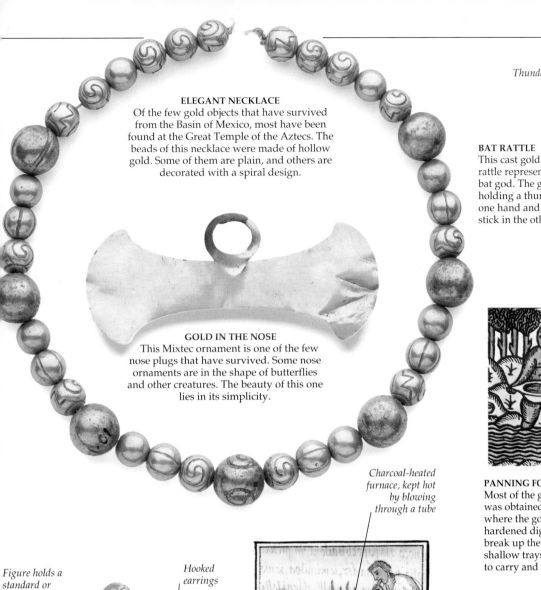

ELEGANT NECKLACE
Of the few gold objects that have survived from the Basin of Mexico, most have been found at the Great Temple of the Aztecs. The beads of this necklace were made of hollow gold. Some of them are plain, and others are decorated with a spiral design.

GOLD IN THE NOSE
This Mixtec ornament is one of the few nose plugs that have survived. Some nose ornaments are in the shape of butterflies and other creatures. The beauty of this one lies in its simplicity.

Thunderbolt

BAT RATTLE
This cast gold rattle represents a bat god. The god is holding a thunderbolt in one hand and a throwing stick in the other.

PANNING FOR GOLD
Most of the gold used by the Peruvian Indians was obtained from "placer" mines in rivers, where the gold is near the surface. They used fire-hardened digging sticks to break up the earth, and shallow trays in which to carry and wash it.

Charcoal-heated furnace, kept hot by blowing through a tube

Figure holds a standard or banner

Hooked earrings

LIME SCOOPS
These tiny lime scoops were used in the preparation of a drug called *coca*. Powdered lime was scooped onto a coca leaf, made into a ball, and chewed.

Handle has figure of a hummingbird

Handle has figure of a monkey

GOLDSMITH
The goldsmith had a high status in Aztec society. He made the most intricate objects using the "lost wax" method. First he made an intricately carved beeswax mould, and carefully covered it with a layer of clay. When it was heated, melted wax flowed out and the mould was filled with molten metal. In this illustration, the goldsmith is about to pour molten gold into a mould.

Llamas were highly valued in the Andean region. Many stylized llama figurines were made

ZAPOTEC GOLD FIGURE
Many gold items seem to depict important people or gods. The items they wear and hold may have had a symbolic meaning for the Mesoamerican people, but we can only guess what it symbolizes. This standing gold figure was probably the work of a Zapotec goldsmith. The figure is wearing a pendant around its neck. Three bells hang from the pendant's head.

GOLD LLAMA
The Incas made vessels and figures using the casting method, by pouring molten metal into a mould. Items like this llama figure were sometimes partly soldered together too.

Precious stones

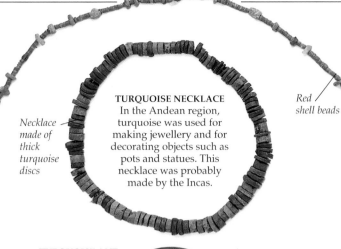

TURQUOISE NECKLACE
In the Andean region, turquoise was used for making jewellery and for decorating objects such as pots and statues. This necklace was probably made by the Incas.

Necklace made of thick turquoise discs

Red shell beads

THE INCAS, MAYAS, AND AZTECS had a taste for all kinds of stones, and their skilled craftsmen fashioned exquisite objects from them. The Incas favoured turquoise which they used as inlay in gold and silver objects. The Mesoamericans favoured stones of different colours with shiny surfaces such as jade and green stones in general, turquoise, onyx, rock crystal, and porphyry (a dark red rock) among others. They made jewellery and a variety of containers, masks, and sculptures. Jade was the most precious material according to the Mesoamerican people. It was associated with water, the life-giving fluid, and with the colour of the maize plant, their staple food. Turquoise was also highly valued and was laboriously worked both in Mesoamerica and in the Andean regions.

TURQUOISE AND GOLD NECKLACE
Turquoise was highly valued in the Andean region. Only a few artefacts, like this delicate Inca necklace, have survived.

CHIMU WOMAN
This Chimu figurine (left) is of a woman wearing a headdress and a necklace strung with various beads, perhaps shells and stones.

Pieces of turquoise

Hollow gold bead

LIKE FATHER, LIKE SON
Craftsmen such as this precious-stone cutter (called a lapidary) passed their skills on to their sons, who would take up their trade on reaching manhood. The Aztecs believed that the arts of the lapidary and the goldsmith came from the Toltecs, who had received their skills from the god *Quetzalcoatl*.

Detail from Codex Mendoza

VAMPIRE BAT
This Zapotec mosaic mask is made of 25 pieces of jade. It is in the shape of a human head covered by a bat's mask. The bat was an important symbol in the art of the Zapotec people.

Eyes made of shell

ONYX CUP
In Mesoamerica, onyx was used for making objects for the elite. The craftsman would begin with a large lump of onyx, cutting out the centre with obsidian tools (above). Many onyx objects are rounded, like this cup (below), as this was the easiest shape to produce.

TURQUOISE MASK *right*
One of the most remarkable Mesoamerican arts was that of mosaic making, especially using turquoise. This mask, representing the god *Quetzalcoatl*, is one of the best preserved examples of Mexican turquoise mosaic.

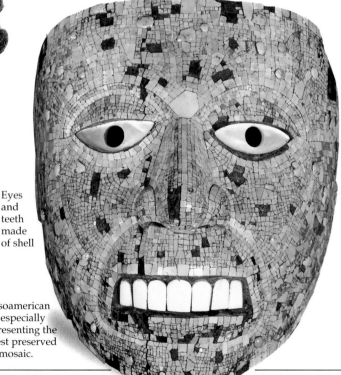

Eyes and teeth made of shell

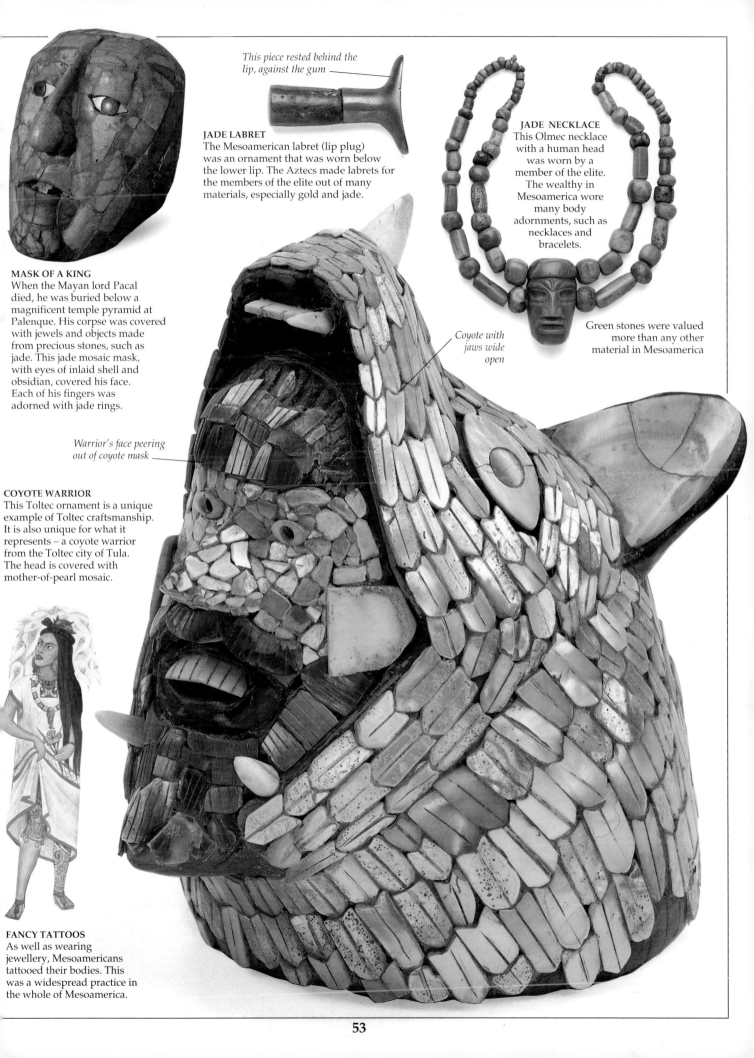

JADE LABRET
The Mesoamerican labret (lip plug) was an ornament that was worn below the lower lip. The Aztecs made labrets for the members of the elite out of many materials, especially gold and jade.

This piece rested behind the lip, against the gum

JADE NECKLACE
This Olmec necklace with a human head was worn by a member of the elite. The wealthy in Mesoamerica wore many body adornments, such as necklaces and bracelets.

Green stones were valued more than any other material in Mesoamerica

MASK OF A KING
When the Mayan lord Pacal died, he was buried below a magnificent temple pyramid at Palenque. His corpse was covered with jewels and objects made from precious stones, such as jade. This jade mosaic mask, with eyes of inlaid shell and obsidian, covered his face. Each of his fingers was adorned with jade rings.

Coyote with jaws wide open

Warrior's face peering out of coyote mask

COYOTE WARRIOR
This Toltec ornament is a unique example of Toltec craftsmanship. It is also unique for what it represents – a coyote warrior from the Toltec city of Tula. The head is covered with mother-of-pearl mosaic.

FANCY TATTOOS
As well as wearing jewellery, Mesoamericans tattooed their bodies. This was a widespread practice in the whole of Mesoamerica.

HUMAN MASK
This finely carved greenstone mask was an offering to the gods, found at the Great Temple of the Aztecs. It is inlaid with shell and obsidian, and its ear lobes are pierced to attach earplugs.

Jade earplug

Masks

FOR HUNDREDS OF YEARS, masks fashioned from materials such as gold, obsidian, jade, and wood – some inlaid with turquoise and coral – have been worn in the Americas. Masks were commonly placed over mummy bundles to protect the deceased from the dangers of the afterlife. They were also worn for festivals. Among the Incas and the Aztecs for whom music and dance (pp. 56–57) were a form of religious expression, masks and costumes had a symbolic meaning. Even today in Mesoamerica and in the Andean region, people still wear masks during festivals.

BEATEN COPPER MASK
Masks such as this copper one (left) have been found on mummies in many Andean burial sites. The wealthier the individual the more elaborate was their burial and the more expensive the fabrics that wrapped and decorated the mummy bundle.

Mask made of stone

Holes in mask may have had hair threaded through them

FACE VALUE
Many objects from the Mezcala region, including masks, were found at the Great Temple of the Aztecs. This mask was paid as tribute to the Aztecs (pp. 26–27).

MAYAN HEAD
Many heads and masks give an idea of what people looked like. This head shows that the Mayas practised cranial deformation, which means that they forced the top of the head to grow taller and slope backwards.

JEWELLED MASK
This Chimu funerary mask is made of thin sheet gold. It would have been placed over a mummy's face. The nose ornament, decorated with gold discs, was made separately.

Eyes decorated with emerald beads

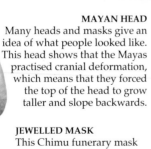

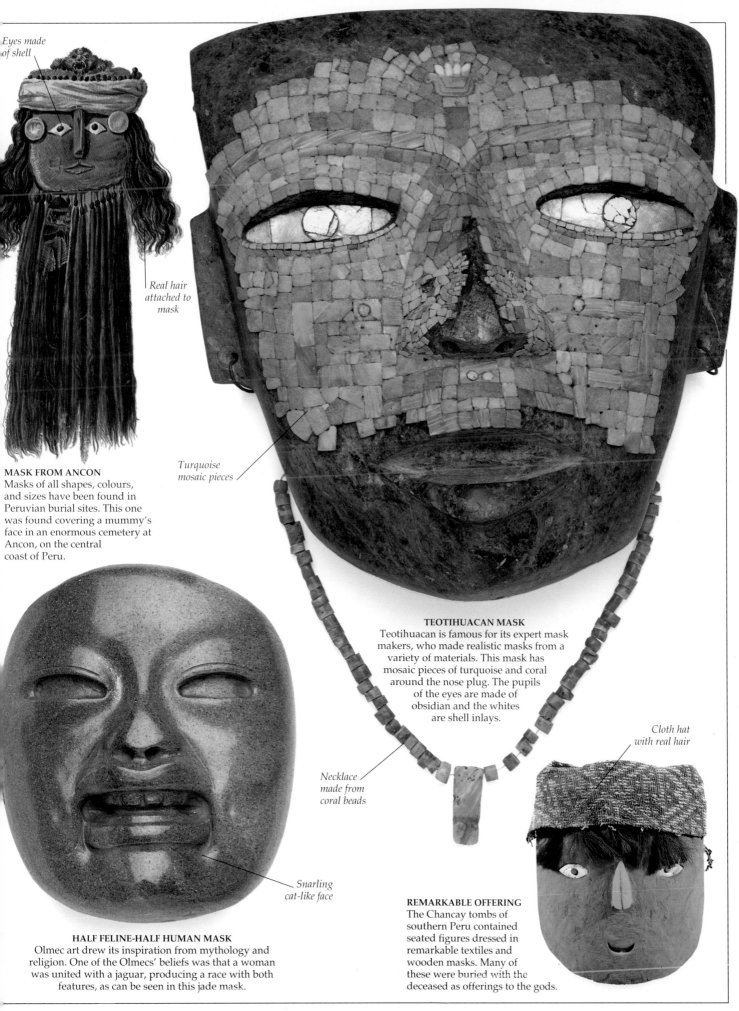

Eyes made of shell

Real hair attached to mask

MASK FROM ANCON
Masks of all shapes, colours, and sizes have been found in Peruvian burial sites. This one was found covering a mummy's face in an enormous cemetery at Ancon, on the central coast of Peru.

Turquoise mosaic pieces

TEOTIHUACAN MASK
Teotihuacan is famous for its expert mask makers, who made realistic masks from a variety of materials. This mask has mosaic pieces of turquoise and coral around the nose plug. The pupils of the eyes are made of obsidian and the whites are shell inlays.

Cloth hat with real hair

Necklace made from coral beads

Snarling cat-like face

HALF FELINE-HALF HUMAN MASK
Olmec art drew its inspiration from mythology and religion. One of the Olmecs' beliefs was that a woman was united with a jaguar, producing a race with both features, as can be seen in this jade mask.

REMARKABLE OFFERING
The Chancay tombs of southern Peru contained seated figures dressed in remarkable textiles and wooden masks. Many of these were buried with the deceased as offerings to the gods.

Music and dance

MOCHE FLAUTIST
Many Moche vases are realistic portraits of people and their pastimes. This one shows that flutes were played in the Andean region.

MUSIC, SONG, AND DANCE were an important part of Mesoamerican and South American life. Scenes of people playing music and dancing decorate many pottery vases, especially those produced by the Moche potters. The most common instruments in both Mesoamerica and South America were rattles, whistles, trumpets, flutes, copper bells, and shells. String instruments were practically unknown in the Americas. The music in South America was not very varied, and often musical instruments only played one tone. For these civilizations, music and dance were closely linked to religion. Everyone, from rulers to peasants, took part in dances especially performed for their gods.

End of rattle in shape of a dog's head

CLAY TRUMPET
Moche trumpets came in straight and coiled shapes. This one ends in two cat-like heads, which may represent a god. This shape of coil is typical of Moche trumpets.

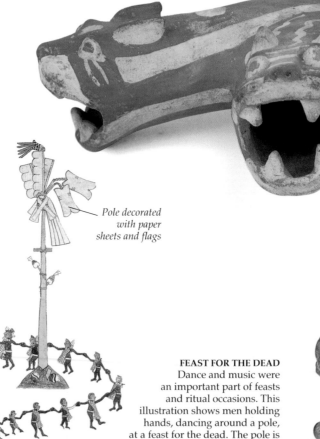

Cat-like heads have gaping, snarling jaws with bared fangs

In Aztec times two types of drum were played – the *huehuetl* or *tlapanhuehuetl* (vertical drum) and the *teponaztli* or horizontal drum

Pole decorated with paper sheets and flags

FEAST FOR THE DEAD
Dance and music were an important part of feasts and ritual occasions. This illustration shows men holding hands, dancing around a pole, at a feast for the dead. The pole is festooned with paper sheets and three big flags, one of which has a feather decoration. The Aztecs adorned an image of the dead person with flags. This feast lasted all day, and people danced to the beat of the drum, played by a priest. The dancers in this illustration were captives who were later burned as sacrifice.

Drum covered with a feline's pelt

INCA PANPIPES

The most commonly played Andean musical instrument was the syrinx or panpipes. They were usually made from cane or pottery. The delicate sounds are produced by blowing across one end of the panpipes. These Inca panpipes are made from the quills of a bird of prey called the condor.

Quills held together by a horizontal quill, tied with string

Panpipes are made of tubes of different lengths

POTTERY RATTLE

Rattles were made of pottery, metal, or strings of large seeds. This Moche rattle has a dog's head at one end. The handle of the rattle is in the shape of a man's head.

Man's head

MUSICAL CELEBRATIONS

Most Inca instruments were wind and percussion instruments. In this fiesta, the women are singing, dancing, and playing the drum, while the men are playing flutes, or *quenas*.

BEATING THE RHYTHM

The horizontal drum, the *teponaztli*, was a hollowed log with a hole in the bottom and slotted at the top; it was played with drumsticks with rubber tips. This codex illustration (right) shows an Aztec orchestra with a similar drum. The decoration of drums varied from intricate carvings to realistic animal or human forms. Some drums were painted or gilded. The carving on this drum is of a person with loose hair, wearing a tasselled headdress decorated with feathers.

AZTEC ORCHESTRA

Gourd (or gourd-shaped) rattles were an essential part of dance. They are depicted in Aztec books and in Maya mural paintings. This illustration shows men shaking rattles and two drummers, one playing the *teponaztli* and the other the *huehuetl*.

UNIQUE FLUTE

The Mesoamerican people played all kinds of flutes, from simple straight ones to more complex ones such as this, decorated with a figure of a woman, standing on a disc that has several openings. This type of flute is unique to Mesoamerica. It was probably played in religious ceremonies.

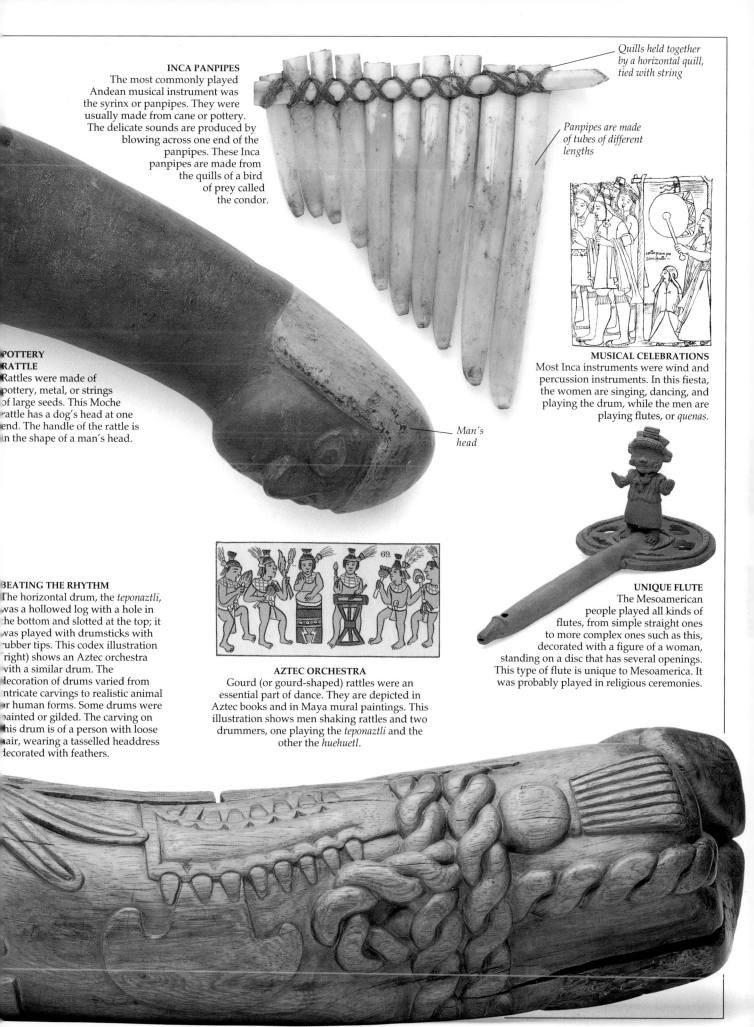

Sports and games

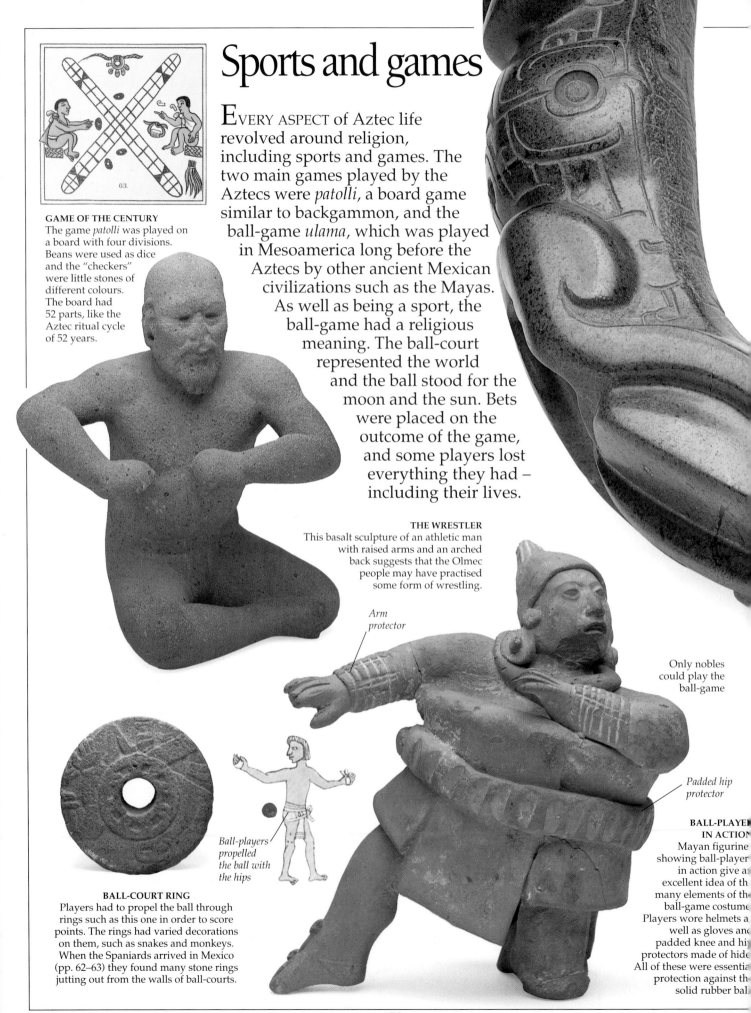

EVERY ASPECT of Aztec life revolved around religion, including sports and games. The two main games played by the Aztecs were *patolli*, a board game similar to backgammon, and the ball-game *ulama*, which was played in Mesoamerica long before the Aztecs by other ancient Mexican civilizations such as the Mayas. As well as being a sport, the ball-game had a religious meaning. The ball-court represented the world and the ball stood for the moon and the sun. Bets were placed on the outcome of the game, and some players lost everything they had – including their lives.

GAME OF THE CENTURY
The game *patolli* was played on a board with four divisions. Beans were used as dice and the "checkers" were little stones of different colours. The board had 52 parts, like the Aztec ritual cycle of 52 years.

THE WRESTLER
This basalt sculpture of an athletic man with raised arms and an arched back suggests that the Olmec people may have practised some form of wrestling.

Arm protector

Only nobles could play the ball-game

Ball-players propelled the ball with the hips

Padded hip protector

BALL-COURT RING
Players had to propel the ball through rings such as this one in order to score points. The rings had varied decorations on them, such as snakes and monkeys. When the Spaniards arrived in Mexico (pp. 62–63) they found many stone rings jutting out from the walls of ball-courts.

BALL-PLAYER IN ACTION
Mayan figurine showing ball-player in action give an excellent idea of the many elements of the ball-game costume. Players wore helmets as well as gloves and padded knee and hip protectors made of hide. All of these were essential protection against the solid rubber ball.

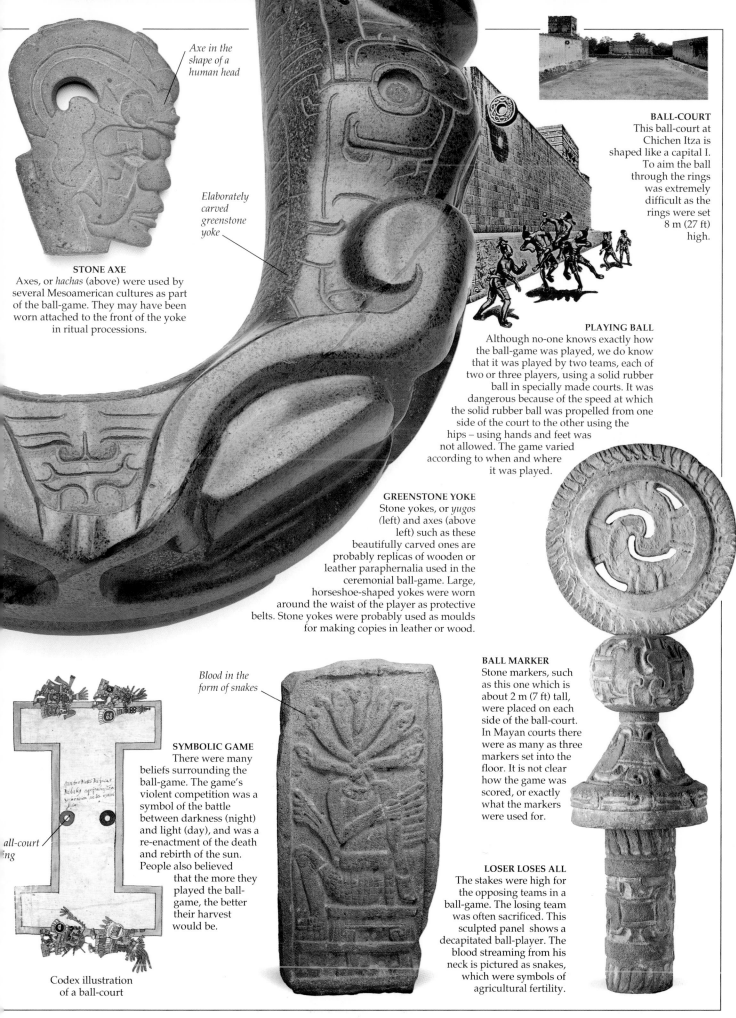

STONE AXE
Axes, or *hachas* (above) were used by several Mesoamerican cultures as part of the ball-game. They may have been worn attached to the front of the yoke in ritual processions.

Axe in the shape of a human head

Elaborately carved greenstone yoke

BALL-COURT
This ball-court at Chichen Itza is shaped like a capital I. To aim the ball through the rings was extremely difficult as the rings were set 8 m (27 ft) high.

PLAYING BALL
Although no-one knows exactly how the ball-game was played, we do know that it was played by two teams, each of two or three players, using a solid rubber ball in specially made courts. It was dangerous because of the speed at which the solid rubber ball was propelled from one side of the court to the other using the hips – using hands and feet was not allowed. The game varied according to when and where it was played.

GREENSTONE YOKE
Stone yokes, or *yugos* (left) and axes (above left) such as these beautifully carved ones are probably replicas of wooden or leather paraphernalia used in the ceremonial ball-game. Large, horseshoe-shaped yokes were worn around the waist of the player as protective belts. Stone yokes were probably used as moulds for making copies in leather or wood.

BALL MARKER
Stone markers, such as this one which is about 2 m (7 ft) tall, were placed on each side of the ball-court. In Mayan courts there were as many as three markers set into the floor. It is not clear how the game was scored, or exactly what the markers were used for.

Blood in the form of snakes

SYMBOLIC GAME
There were many beliefs surrounding the ball-game. The game's violent competition was a symbol of the battle between darkness (night) and light (day), and was a re-enactment of the death and rebirth of the sun. People also believed that the more they played the ball-game, the better their harvest would be.

all-court ng

Codex illustration of a ball-court

LOSER LOSES ALL
The stakes were high for the opposing teams in a ball-game. The losing team was often sacrificed. This sculpted panel shows a decapitated ball-player. The blood streaming from his neck is pictured as snakes, which were symbols of agricultural fertility.

Bestiary

ANIMAL LIFE in the Americas was very rich and varied. Animals played an important part in everyday life as well as in the religions of both regions. Many works of art are decorated with images of animals that were significant to them – for example foxes, owls, hummingbirds, jaguars, eagles, and llamas. Some animals were domesticated – the turkey and the dog in Mesoamerica, and the llama and the alpaca in the Andean region. With their relatives, guanacos and vicunas, llamas and alpacas were valued for their wool, meat, or as beasts of burden. In both regions, deer, rabbits, ducks, and many other kinds of edible bird abounded. Animal life in the tropical forests included the largest cat in the world, the jaguar, which was worshipped and feared along with snakes.

BIRD ASSORTMENT
Mesoamerica had a variety of brilliantly coloured tropical birds such as parrots, macaws, and quetzals. Their feathers were used to decorate many objects and clothes (pp. 48–49).

QUETZAL BIR
This bird was greatl valued by the ancien Mesoamericans, fo whom its long, dee green feathers were a precious as jade c gold. Some of thei gods were covered i quetzal feathers, an they were also used t make the headdresse of rulers and king

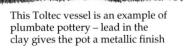

This Toltec vessel is an example of plumbate pottery – lead in the clay gives the pot a metallic finish

BIRD TAPESTRY *above*
The Paracas culture is renowned for its abundant, ornate textiles that were placed alongside the dead. This textile fragment is decorated with a typical Paracas design of stylized birds.

Figure has cat-like claws and ears and a monkey's tail

FABRIC "DEVIL"
Many textiles from Paracas are woven or embroidered with animal images, often in a stylized form. Sometimes it is difficult to identify the animal in question, because of the geometric forms.

FO
Animals such as the fo that hunted and kille other animals, were i turn hunte by the Aztec and the Inca This Moch vessel is i the shape of snarling fo

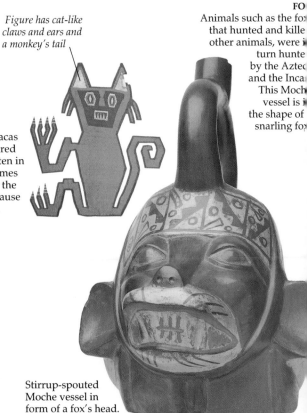

TOLTEC CERAMIC DOG
Some breeds of dog were fattened and eaten by the Aztecs and the Mayas, but the Incas found eating dog meat a disgusting habit. The Mesoamericans used dogs as companions in hunting expeditions. According to their religion, dogs were also necessary for the journey to the afterlife as they helped the dead cross rivers.

Stirrup-spouted Moche vessel in form of a fox's head.

Vicunas live on the grasslands of the Andean mountains

Vicunas reach a height of 80 cm (30 in) at the shoulder

ARMADILLO
The Aztecs ate the meat of the armadillo, which is white and tastes like chicken. Among the Mayas, the armadillo was associated with the afterlife.

Some armadillos grow to a length of 120 cm (4 ft)

The armadillo is a nocturnal mammal that lives in tropical areas

ALPACA
The alpaca lives in the Andean highlands. It was kept in herds by the ancient Peruvians because, along with the vicuna, its long wool was ideal for weaving. Its relatives the guanaco and the llama were killed for food, although the llama was mostly used for carrying loads. The ancient Andean people made offerings to this animal as it was an important contribution to their livelihood.

VICUNAS
Like the alpaca, the vicuna (above) was a good wool-producing animal. Vicunas had the most elegant silk-like wool. Garments woven from vicuna wool were worn by the Inca nobility.

Zapotec vessel probably used as an incense burner

Ocelot

OCELOT
This wild cat is sometimes known as the Mexican tiger. The ocelot was a greatly feared creature. Some warriors wore ocelot skins when going to battle.

Jaguars, ocelots, and pumas lived in tropical forests

Puma

PUMA
The puma is a native animal to the Americas. It was hunted for its skin.

Jaguar

SACRED JAGUAR
The jaguar was one of the most powerful symbols in Mesoamerica and South America. Its strength, ferocity, cunning, and hunting ability were greatly admired. This Zapotec vessel (far right) is in the shape of a jaguar standing on three legs.

Leg decorated with head of baby jaguar

The Spanish conquest

WHEN THE SPANISH ARRIVED in the Americas, they knew nothing about the Andean and Mesoamerican cultures with their powerful empires, elaborate palaces, magnificent engineering works, and religions that reached into every part of their life. Neither did the inhabitants of the Americas have any knowledge of the Spanish. Many omens had forewarned Moctezuma, the Aztec ruler, of an imminent disaster. The Inca ruler Huayna Capac, too, had heard that strange, bearded men had appeared on the coast. When Cortés entered Mexico in 1519 and Pizarro arrived in Peru in 1532, they easily overpowered resistance. Despite being few in number the Spanish armies, with their horses and cannons, were stronger. Cortés had the added advantage that the Aztecs believed him to be the king and god *Quetzalcoatl*. Within a short time, the world of the Aztecs and the Incas was destroyed, their temples razed to the ground, and their emperors murdered. The Mayas resisted until 1542, when the Spanish established a capital at Mérida.

MOCTEZUMA GREETS CORTÉS
When they first met, Cortés greeted Moctezuma with a bow, and Moctezum handed him splendid presents of gold, precious stones such as jade, and feathe objects. Cortés was on horseback and Moctezuma was carried in a litter. The Spanish soldiers were dressed in steel armour while the Aztecs wore simple cotton cloaks. This meeting would prov decisive in the conquest of Mexico. Moctezuma at this point was in two minds about the true nature of Cortés – was he human or god, their enemy or their saviour? The events that followed proved Cortés to be the former.

MASSACRE
The conquistadors went in search of riches. If they met with resistance from the native people, the conquistadors killed them. This illustration depicts an expedition to Michoacan in the west of Mexico, where many local noblemen were killed for refusing to say where their treasures were hidden.

Warriors from the state of Tlaxcala supported the conquistadors

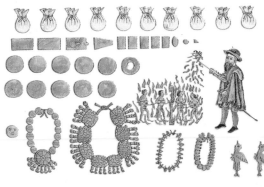

GOLDEN DEATH
This scene from Codex Kingsborough shows a Spanish tribute collector punishing the Mexican Indians at Tepetlaoztoc. A Spanish tribute collector was known as an *encomendero* (privileged Spanish colonist). The Indians being burned were late in paying their tribute. The tribute demanded consisted of bundles of maize and gold jewellery.

Gold doubloons made from gold mined in South America

A DISEASE THAT ONLY GOLD COULD CURE

To coerce the people of Middle and South America to give them their gold, the Spanish often told them that they suffered from a disease that only gold could cure. Cortés and Pizarro both went to the Americas in search of gold and they found much of it. At the start of the conquest, Cortés sent booty to King Charles V of Spain consisting of gold and silver objects and many other goods. Over the years, huge quantities of gold were shipped to Spain. Today the ceilings of many Spanish churches are gilded with gold from the Americas.

PUNISHMENT

This illustration shows some of the punishments used by the Spanish on the Inca people. They included beating them and hanging them upside down. The cruelty of many of the conquistadors made some Spanish friars devote their life to denouncing the behaviour of their compatriots.

Francisco Pizarro, conquistador of Peru

Wooden Inca beaker, possibly made for Pizarro himself

GREED FOR GOLD

This caricature shows a greedy Francisco Pizarro, contemplating gold from his new Peruvian mine. Pizarro did not understand the civilization that he helped to destroy.

CONQUISTADOR'S BEAKER

This wooden *kero* (p. 50) portrays the conquistador of Peru, Francisco Pizarro. Under Pizarro, Spanish control was established over the Inca empire. They forced people to abandon their irrigated lands, and demanded that they mine more precious metals. Christianity was imposed upon the Incas, but they were slow to accept the new religion and continued in their old practices. The Incas continued with some of their crafts, such as weaving and making wooden *keros* like this one.

Did you know?

Both the Mayas and the Aztecs were excellent beekeepers. They raised stingless bees for honey, which was harvested once a year for medicine and for sweetening food.

Chewing gum may have been an Aztec innovation. The chicozapote tree, one of the most common in Mesoamerica, produces a resin called "chicle," from which chewing gum is made. The Aztecs chewed on chicle to clean their teeth.

Chicozapote tree

The Mayan people had a zodiac of constellations made up of animals. These included the turtle, the bat, the jaguar, and the turkey. The only animal common to both Mayan and Western zodiac signs is the scorpion.

The Aztecs used a beverage made from live toads steeped in sugar in some of their religious rituals. Toads in the *Bufo* genus secrete toxins from their parotid glands which, when consumed, have hallucinogenic powers. Many Aztec medicines were based on these secretions.

Some Mayan temples featured a complex mosaic of stonework around the entrance door that gave the impression of the jaws of a monster, including stone snouts and fangs. This is because, in Mayan belief, the entrance to the underworld was thought of as the mouth of a monster. By entering a temple decorated in this way, priests believed they were literally stepping into the supernatural world.

Mayan temple entrance resembling jaws

Many Inca kings kept everything they had contact with, so that they could be buried with it. Tombs have been found containing hampers of used clothing, the king's dishes and cutlery, hair and nail clippings – even corn cobs and old bones once gnawed on by the king.

In Mesoamerica, the jaguar (the largest cat of the Americas) was a symbol of royal power. Kings wore the jaguar's pelt as part of their regalia, and jaguars were offered to the gods in sacrifice.

The Mayas believed that slightly crossed eyes were beautiful. They dangled objects in front of their eyes in an attempt to cross them. Foreheads that sloped back were also considered beautiful. To achieve this, the Mayas tied boards to babies' foreheads to mould their skulls into the desired shape. This process did not seem to harm the brain.

The Aztec Calendar Stone, carved in the early 16th century, is immense. It measures over 4 m (13 ft) in diameter and weighs 24 tonnes. The Aztec solar year contained 18 months of 20 days each, with 5 extra days. Aztec priests used the calendar to keep track of important festival dates. The face of the stone contains various mythological and astrological figures and signs. The most important figure in the stone is *Tonatiuh*, the sun god, located in the centre.

Mayan artists, unlike those of many ancient cultures, often included their names on stone carvings and other works. There are also Mayan ceramics "signed" with the artist's name.

The large number and wide variety of musical instruments found in archaeological sites in Mesoamerica shows the important place of music and dance in cultural life. There were drums made of wood or clay topped with monkey skins; rattles made of turtle shells; hollow shakers filled with shells, seeds, or dried llama toenails; conch shell trumpets; and flutes made from animal and human bones.

Flute

Clothing was an important status symbol among the Incas. The king had certain fabrics reserved for his use alone. His shirts were of the finest, most delicate cloth, embroidered with gold and silver and decorated with bird feathers. Some royal clothing was made of such difficult-to-produce fibres as bat hair.

Figures from mythology are shown on the calendar stone

Modern reconstruction of Aztec calendar

QUESTIONS AND ANSWERS

Q Why was the ball game *ulama* so important?

A The Mesoamericans were absolutely obsessed with *ulama*, not only as a sport played for general recreation, but as a religious ritual. The game between competing teams of players may have symbolized the battles between the sky gods and the lords of the underworld, with the ball itself representing the sun. In some games, the leader of a losing team was decapitated; his skull then formed the core of a new ball. In other games, the winning team's prize was to behead the unfortunate players of the losing team.

Disc inlaid in Mayan ball-court floor

Q What was in the water at the Sacred Cenote at Chichen Itza?

A Cenotes (natural wells formed after the roof of an underground river collapses) were important to the Mayas. They considered them a way to communicate directly with *Chac*, the god of water, to ask for plentiful rain for the crops. For hundreds of years, people told tales of fabulous gold and jade objects tossed into these wells to appease *Chac*. An American consul to the region named Edward Thompson used his diplomatic skills to purchase the lands containing the Sacred Cenote at Chichen Itza. Between 1904 and 1907, he hired men to dive into the murky waters and used a simple dredge to pull up hundreds of precious objects (and child-sized human bones). Many of these were taken out of the country and displayed in the Peabody Museum in Boston, the United States; the Mexican authorities fought for decades for the return of the treasures, which are now on display in the Regional Museum in Merida, Mexico.

Q Where was the City of the Gods, and why was it sacred to the Aztecs?

A The ruins of the city of Teotihuacan, an ancient religious capital of the Aztecs, lie just north of present-day Mexico City. The city dates back to around 100 B.C. Two huge step pyramids, the Pyramid of the Sun and the Pyramid of the Moon, dominated the city centre. The Aztecs believed that the city was where the gods gathered to create the sun and the moon, and made it a pilgrimage centre. By about A.D. 500 it was the largest city in the Americas (and the site of thousands of sacrifices).

View of Teotihuacan ruins along the Avenue of the Dead

Q Who rediscovered Machu Picchu, the lost city of the Incas?

A This incredible city was constructed by the Incas sometime around 1440, and was inhabited until the Spanish conquest of Peru. Its large palace and temples surrounding a courtyard were not meant to be a "working" city, but a country retreat for the Inca nobility. American historian Hiram Bingham, in the area to explore old Inca roads, encountered the city in 1911. He wrote a number of books and articles that introduced Machu Picchu to the rest of the world.

Q What is the mystery behind the Nazca lines in Peru?

A The Nazca people created hundreds of pictures in the Peruvian desert of birds, insects, mammals, fish, and plants. These immense "drawings" were made by arranging small stones on the desert flats. They may have been sacred pathways, as some of the lines meet at small shrines where offerings were made.

Q What happened to the Mesoamericans after the Spanish conquests?

A Many people were captured and killed by the conquistadors; scores of others died from contact with new European diseases. The Spanish and Portuguese who conquered the area also enslaved people, sending them to mine precious metals. It is important to note that the people did not simply disappear. While Aztec, Inca, and Maya are generally used as historical terms, millions of their descendants still live in the region, and speak related languages.

Record Breakers

OLDEST INTACT MAYAN MURAL
In 2002, archaeologist William Saturno uncovered a near-pristine Mayan mural dating from A.D. 100, in San Bartolo, Guatemala.

LARGEST BALL COURT IN MESOAMERICA
The court at Chichen Itza measures 168 m (551 ft) long and 70 m (229 ft) wide. Its acoustics are so precise that you can stand on one end and hear people talking at the other.

TALLEST MAYAN PYRAMID
The Temple of the Jaguar in Tikal, Guatemala, erected around A.D. 741, rises 65 m (212 ft) high.

LARGEST ADOBE STRUCTURE IN MESOAMERICA
The Temple of the Sun in Peru has a square base, measuring 223 m (730 ft) on each side. Originally it rose to 70 m (200 ft) in height.

LARGEST PREHISTORIC REPRESENTATION OF A HUMAN FIGURE IN THE WORLD
The geoglyph of the Giant of Atacama, located in Iquique, Chile, is 86 m (282 ft) long.

Nazca bird figure in the deserts of Peru

Timeline

THE SPANISH EXPLORERS WHO REACHED THE AMERICAS in the 16th century may have called it the "New World," but the lands they described were already home to amazing civilizations that had risen and thrived for centuries. These were the Mesoamerican cultures of the Aztecs and the Mayas, and the South American culture of the Incas. The people among the tribes and nations of these cultures built spectacular cities, created masterpieces of art, established trading links, created religious traditions, and built vast political empires. This timeline will guide you through the cultural history of these regions of the Americas.

Moche owl figure

c. 13,000 B.C.

Asian hunter-gatherers probably make the first crossings into Alaska and the Yukon in North America over the Bering Strait; by c. 11,000 B.C. there are people in Chile.

c. 7000 B.C.

The first crops are grown in Mexico. Maize is first cultivated there c. 5,000 B.C.

c. 3500 B.C.

The llama is first used as a pack animal in Peru; it is also used as a food source.

c. 3500 B.C.

Cotton is first introduced as a crop in Peruvian villages. Women weave sturdy cloth from the cotton and are often buried with their weaving baskets.

1500 B.C.– A.D. 300

The extent of the Preclassic Period; the Olmecs dominate.

Cotton

c. 1200 B.C.

The rise of the Olmec civilization on the coast of the Gulf of Mexico. The Olmecs (believed to be the first civilization in North and Central America) thrive for 600 years. They are skilled artisans as well as fishermen, farmers, and traders.

c. 600 B.C.

The Oaxaca culture begins to overtake the Olmec culture. The Zapotec civilization is established with its capital in Monte Alban.

c. 500 B.C.

The Paracas culture flourishes in Peru. The people are skilled at embroidery, using over a hundred shades of colour to fashion their elaborate works.

c. 200 B.C.

The Nazca culture begins in southern Peru; its people are known for painted pottery as well as for creating large and mysterious geoglyphs in the desert. This date also marks the beginning of the early Classic period of the Maya in central America.

c. A.D. 100

The Moche civilization on the Peruvian coast begins. The Moche are excellent potters and the first South Americans to produce clay objects from moulds. The people are also highly skilled weavers and goldsmiths.

c. A.D. 250

The Maya civilization begins in Guatemala, Honduras, and eastern Mexico. The Mayas do not have a capital city or single ruler. Instead, each city governs itself. The Mayas dominate the Classic Period.

A.D. 300–750

The extent of the Classic Period in Mesoamerican cultural history.

c. A.D. 600

The Tiahuanaco empire grows near Lake Titicaca in Bolivia. Its people establish a leading trading centre, the vast city of Teotihuacan, which becomes home to over 100,000 people. Their Peruvian neighbours, the Huari, share their religion and art styles, and together the two cultures control the entire Andean region.

c. A.D. 650

The Pyramid of the Sun is the centre of civilization for the mighty Teotihuacan culture in Mexico. It is part of a large complex, linked by wide, straight streets, and includes three pyramids, palaces, warrior schools, shrines to the gods of war and rain, and a ball court.

Pyramid of the Sun, Teotihuacan

c. A.D. 850
The Maya civilization in the southern part of Mexico begins to fade. Over the next 200 years, Mayan control of northern Mexico also wanes. Battling empires emerge to take control of the region.

c. A.D. 900–1000
The Toltecs build a capital at Tula, Mexico. Their culture blends many aspects of Mayan culture with their own. They are excellent architects and artisans, and worship *Quetzalcoatl* (the "Feathered Serpent") as a man-god. The Toltecs eventually settle in Chichen Itza and build amazing pyramids there.

c. A.D. 900
The small kingdom of the Chancay flourishes on the central coast of Peru. Its people develop a distinctive pottery style.

Chimu gold spoon

c. 1000
The Chimu culture is on the rise in Peru. Its people are skilled goldsmiths, weavers, and architects. They build their capital at Chan Chan, on the coast. The Chimu are eventually conquered by Inca warriors.

c. 1300
The Incas begin to expand their empire throughout the central Andes. They are ruled by Viracocha, the first major Inca empire builder.

c. 1325
The Aztecs found the city of Tenochtitlan (present-day Mexico City) on an island in Lake Texcoco.

c. 1400–1470
Both the Aztec and Inca empires expand rapidly. In 1426, the Aztecs make an alliance with neighbouring cities to help concentrate power in Aztec emperor Itzcoatl's hands. They establish a vast trading empire, and build spectacular temples and pyramids. By 1500 there are more than 10 million Aztec citizens. The Inca empire is also growing. Around 1438, Viracocha dies; his successor Pachacuti expands the Inca empire north to present-day Ecuador. The Incas develop a massive road network covering more than 30,000 km (19,000 miles). Relay runners stationed along the network carry urgent messages and military orders back and forth along the entire route.

1440–1468
Aztec emperor Moctezuma I and his army take control of large areas of eastern Mexico.

c. 1450
The Incan city of Machu Picchu is built on a remote mountain ridge above the Urubamba River in Peru.

1455
A huge temple is built to the Aztec war god *Huizilopochtli* in Tenochtitlan.

1470
The collapse of the Chimu culture in northern Peru

1486–1502
The rule of the Aztec emperor Ahuitzotl. The Aztec empire is at its height of power in Mexico under his reign.

1513
Spanish explorer Vasco de Balboa first sights the Pacific Ocean, setting the stage for the arrival of the Spanish conquistadors.

Cortés

1519
Spanish explorer and soldier Hernándo Cortés and a band of 500 men reach the Aztec capital of Tenochtitlan. The Aztec emperor Moctezuma greets him as an honoured guest, but Cortés betrays him, arresting him and killing hundreds of Aztec nobles. The remaining Aztecs revolt the following year, but Cortés eventually prevails, and the Aztec empire falls.

1532–1533
With fewer than 200 armed soldiers fighting alongside him, the Spanish warrior Francisco Pizarro attacks the Inca emperor Atahualpa as he marches with his entourage to his coronation. Everyone is killed apart from Atahualpa; his life is spared on the condition that he pay a ransom in silver and gold. He hands over the treasure and is promptly strangled.

1542
The Spanish establish a capital at Merida, and the Mayan resistance comes to an end.

1615
Felipe Guaman Poma de Ayala, a native Incan, completes his 1,200-page work, *The First New Chronicle and Good Government*, illustrated with 400 pen-and-ink drawings of Inca and colonial life. He addresses the work to King Philip III of Spain, hoping to seek reform of Spanish colonial governance in order to save the Andean peoples from the destructive forces of colonialism.

Page from Guaman Poma's book

Guaman Poma used drawings in his book, such as this one of a patient visiting a healer, because he felt that pictures were as persuasive as words

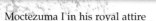
Moctezuma I in his royal attire

Find out more

THE CULTURES OF THE AZTEC, INCA, AND MAYA may have disappeared, but the wealth of relics and ruins left behind reveal much about these ancient people and their times. If you are able to visit Central or South America, you can explore the sites of these once-thriving cities and follow in the footsteps of the people who lived there. But there are plenty of other ways to learn more about these cultures. The Internet offers virtual tours of places such as ancient temples and sacred cities. Many museums contain excellent collections from these areas.

ENJOY A TREAT TO EAT
If you are hungry to learn more about the cultures you have read about in this book, try a taste of traditional Central and South American cuisine. Many restaurants feature foods based on the same staples – maize, squash, and beans – that fed the Aztec, Inca, and Maya people. Try your hand at cooking a traditional dish, such as tacos.

THE INCA TRAIL TO MACHU PICCHU
Many of the sites sacred to the ancient Americans are now popular tourist destinations. For example, you can trek along the Inca Trail in Peru to the sacred city of Machu Picchu, thought to be the oldest city in the Americas. The Spanish invaders at the time of the conquest and during centuries of colonial rule had no idea the city was even there. The city is now a World Heritage site and has thousands of visitors a day.

THE SOUNDS OF THE PAST
Music was an important part of ancient South American and Mesoamerican religious rituals. Today, folk musicians keep the sounds of the past alive, performing traditional music on modern replicas of instruments used by Aztec, Inca, and Maya musicians. These musicians perform in traditional costume. Check the Internet to find out if a group will be performing at a cultural festival near you.

USEFUL WEBSITES

www.mesoweb.com
Explore the cultures of Mesoamerica

www.ancientmexico.com
The history of ancient Mexico, with an interactive map

www.ancientperu.com
An in-depth look at the Inca universe

www.pbs.org/conquistadors
The story of Spain's crusading adventurers

www.ballgame.org
The Mesoamerican ball-game brought vividly to life

Places to Visit

THE BRITISH MUSEUM, LONDON
The museum's gallery devoted to pre-Hispanic cultures in Mesoamerica includes Mixtec codices, sculptures, and a famous collection of Mixtec-Aztec turquoise mosaics.

WORLD MUSEUM, LIVERPOOL
In this museum's world cultures gallery, visitors can see pages from the Codex Fejérváry-Mayer, one of the few surviving codices that dates before the destruction of Tenochtitlan. It also includes jewellery, sculptures, and artefacts from the Mayan culture.

MUSEUM OF ARCHAEOLOGY AND ANTHROPOLOGY, CAMBRIDGE
This museum includes objects from the Moche, Nazca, and Chimu cultures.

MUSEO NACIONAL DE ANTROPOLOGÍA, MEXICO CITY, MEXICO
This museum contains possibly the world's greatest collection of objects related to the Maya. Its interactive kiosks tell the stories behind some 500 important objects on display.

METROPOLITAN MUSEUM OF ART, NEW YORK, UNITED STATES
The museum's collection from the ancient Americas spans a 3,500 year period, and includes the world's most comprehensive collection of American gold.

AZTEC DANCERS
Traditional Aztec dance troupes wear vivid costumes lavished with gold and silver embroidery, and elaborate feather headdresses. These dancers are performing at a Native American heritage festival in the United States. Check listings or the Internet to find out if any traditional dance troupes are making an international tour.

VISIT A MUSEUM
Many art and anthropology museums feature important works from the Aztec, Inca, and Maya civilizations. A museum collection might include examples of textiles, pottery, metalwork, featherwork, basketry, and artefacts crafted from precious stones. Check with travel books or use the Internet to find the best permanent collections (some of which are listed in the box, top right). Also look out for travelling exhibitions from museums in Central and South America.

TRAVEL TO ANCIENT SITES
Exploring the lands of the Aztec, Inca, or Maya can be awe-inspiring. These tourists are climbing a pyramid in Mexico. Use the Internet to find sites open to visitors. Joining a group tour may give you access to more sites, as well as a valuable commentary from tour guides.

Glossary

ADOBE A traditional building material made from clay, straw, and water, formed into blocks and dried.

AGAVE A tropical American plant with tough, sword-shaped leaves and flowers in tall spikes. In Mesoamerica, the plant's fibres were woven into cloth; people also sucked the sap directly from the plant.

Agave plant

ALPACA A member of the llama family from the South American Andes Mountains. Alpaca hair fibre is prized for the soft, lightweight, yet extremely warm wool that can be woven from it.

ARMADILLO A burrowing, nocturnal mammal covered in strong, horny plates; eaten by Mesoamerican peoples.

ATOLE A mush or thin porridge made with maize, popular in Mesoamerica. The Incas ate a similar dish, called *capia*.

CACAO A tropical evergreen tree. Its dried and partially fermented beans are removed from their pods and processed to make chocolate, cocoa powder, and cocoa butter.

CALPULLI An Aztec neighbourhood with shared rights and responsibilities among the households. The *calpulli* was the basic unit of Aztec society.

CHACMOOL A Mesoamerican sculpture of a reclining figure holding a bowl on its lap or stomach. The bowl is thought to be a receptacle for holding blood and human hearts after a sacrifice.

CHASQUIS In Moche society, a runner who carried messages from one place to another.

CHINAMPAS In Aztec agriculture, narrow strips of land built in swampy lakes, with canals between them. Each chinampa was built with layers of plants cut from the lake, and fertile soil from the lake bed.

CODEX An ancient type of book made from folded sheets of bark sewn together; the name comes from *caudex*, which is the Latin word for tree bark.

COMAL A large clay disc used for cooking tortillas over an open fire.

CONQUEST The acquisition of a territory and its people by force.

CONQUISTADOR One of the 16th-century Spanish explorers who conquered lands in the Americas.

COPAL A brittle, aromatic resin burned as an incense offering in ancient times; now used in varnishes.

DOUBLOON An old Spanish gold coin.

EMBROIDERY The act of embellishing a fabric or garment with a decorative pattern using hand-stitched needlework.

ENCOMENDERO A privileged Spanish colonist during the Spanish conquest of the Americas. The *encomenderos* became an early colonial aristocracy.

FRESCO From the Italian word for "fresh," the technique of painting on wet plaster so that the pigments are absorbed by the plaster, becoming part of the wall itself. A form of fresco was employed by the artisans of Teotihuacan.

FUNERARY MASK A mask, typically made of metal, that was sometimes placed on the faces of Inca mummies before burial.

Mesoamerican glyph carved in stone

GLYPH A picture used to represent a word or a group of words.

GOURD Any of a group of inedible, vine-growing fruits with hard rinds.

GREENSTONE A dark green metamorphic rock that owes its colouring to the presence of the mineral chlorite.

HIEROGLYPHIC WRITING A system of writing in which the characters consist of realistic or stylized pictures of actual objects, animals, or humans, rather than letters or words.

HUACAS In the Andean regions, a variety of shrines and objects and the natural forces associated with them.

Detail from *Codex Cospi*, an Aztec calendar, showing a god attacking an ocelot warrior

JAGUAR A large, spotted feline of tropical America, similar to the leopard.

KERO A drinking vessel, made of metal or wood, traditionally used in Andean feasts.

LABRET A plug inserted through a piercing in the lip.

Jade labret from Mesoamerica

LOOM A machine used to weave yarn into a fabric.

MAGUEY A type of agave plant.

MAIZE A tall annual cereal grass bearing kernels on large ears of corn; a staple in Mexico, and Central and South America.

MAQUAHUITL One of the Aztecs' main weapons; a wooden club edged with sharp obsidian blades.

MESOAMERICA The region of Mexico and Central America historically inhabited by the Aztecs, Maya, and related cultures.

METLATL A grinding stone, usually made from volcanic stone such as basalt. *Metlatl* were commonly found in the Mesoamerican kitchen, and are still used today.

MUMMY A body embalmed and dried and wrapped for burial.

MUMMY BUNDLE A Mesoamerican mummy wrapped in textiles or reed matting and tied with ropes.

Incan mummy bundle

OBSIDIAN A volcanic glass that may be clear, black, brown, or green. Obsidian is a prized material for making tools, because it can be chipped into a sharp point.

OCELOT A natural wildcat of Central and South America with a dark-spotted brown coat.

ONYX A semiprecious stone that is black and white and arranged in layers.

PATOLLI An Aztec board game that is very similar to modern-day backgammon.

PECCARY A nocturnal, pig-like wild animal of North and South America.

PONCHO A blanket-like cloak, with a slit in the middle for the head.

PYRAMID A massive memorial with a square base and four triangular sides.

QUETZAL A large tropical bird of Central and South America with golden-green and scarlet feathers.

QUETZALCOATL A legendary plumed or feathered serpent, worshipped by the Mayas as a god of nature.

QUINOA A tiny, round, ivory-coloured whole grain used by the Incas, and still eaten today. It is a complete source of dietary protein.

QUIPU An Incan counting device consisting of a length of cord held horizontally, with various knotted strings hanging down. Information was recorded according to the number of knots tied in the strings.

RITUAL The name for any customary observance or practice common to a people.

SACRIFICE The act of killing an animal or person in order to please a deity.

SARCOPHAGUS A stone container that usually housed a coffin and a mummy.

SPINDLE A stick or pin used to twist the yarn in spinning wool.

TEMPLE A religious structure built for the worship of a deity.

TERRACING In agriculture, a series of levels on a hillside, one above the other, used to greatly reduce the water erosion of soil.

TERRACOTTA An unglazed fired clay, used for architectural features, ornaments, vessels, and in creating sculpture.

TURQUOISE An opaque, blue, semiprecious stone with a porous, soft texture, prized in Mesoamerica.

TZOMPANTLI A skull rack placed outside a temple to hold the skulls of victims of sacrifice, for example.

UICTLI An essential farmer's tool, a digging stick made from strong, long-lasting wood with a long, broad blade carved into one end.

Tzompantli at Chichen Itza

ULAMA The sacred ball game, played in Mesoamerica by ancient civilizations as well as the Aztecs.

VICUNA A small, wild, cud-chewing animal similar to a llama but smaller; valued for its fleecy coat.

VIGESIMAL Relating to, or based on, the number 20, as in Mayan mathematics.

WHORL A circular arrangement of three or more leaves or flowers, equally spaced around the stem like spokes on a wheel.

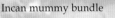

The long, flowing tail feathers were prized for use in religious ceremonies

Quetzal

Index

Acknowledgements

The publisher would like to thank:
Dra. Mari Carmen Serra Puche and all those who helped with photography at Museo Nacional de Antropología, Mexico City; Professor Eduardo Matos Moctezuma and all those who helped with photography at the Great Temple Museum, Mexico City (INAH.-CNCA.-Mex); Phil Watson at the Birmingham Museum; Maureen Barry at the Royal Museum of Scotland; British Museum; Pitt Rivers Museum; Cambridge University Museum of Archaeology and Anthropology; Reynaldo Izquierdo (Mexico) and Eugene Staken for photographic assistance; sue giles at the City of Bristol Museum; Jabu Mahlangu, Manisha Patel, Jill Plank, and Sharon Spencer for design assistance; Katharine Thompson; Lic. Victor Hugo Vidal Alvarez and Lic. Javier García Martinez at the Tourist Office, Mexico City; Lynn Bresler for the index; John Woodcock and Andrew Nash for illustrations.

Additional photography: Geoff Dann (24ar); Steve Gorton (39al); Peter Hayman (60cl; 60c); Dave King (61bc); James Stephenson (14bl; 62-63 top; 63bl); Jerry Young (61ar; 61cl).

Picture credits
a=above, b=below, c-centre, l-left, r=right

Archaeological Museum, Lima/e.t. archive: 20bl, 38br, 51br, 55br; Arteaga Collection, Lima/ e/t/ archive: 15cr; Biblioteca Medicea Laurenziana, Florence: 14acl, 48al, 51c; Biblioteca Nacional, Madrid/Bridgeman Art Library: 62cl; Biblioteca Nazionale Centrale, Florence 21al/Photo-Scala: 35cl, 37al; Bibliothèque de l'Assemblée nationale, Paris: 30bl, 56bl; Bristol Museums and Art Gallery: 29br, 46c, 49bl, 62br; British Library/Bridgeman Art Library: 17c, 19al; British Museum/Bridgeman Art Library: 54bl; J.L. Charmet: 37bl, 44bl; Bruce Coleman Ltd: 16ar, 19ar, 60ar, 61al, 61cl; Dorig/Hutchison Library: 7ar, 30cl, 34a; e.t. archive: 22c, 32al, 38c, 40cr, 51br, 57c, 58al; Mary Evans Picture Library 33cl, 45ac, 62bl/Explorer: 40al; Robert Harding Picture Library: 11bl, 17ac, 18cr, 18bl; Michael Holford: 16c, 17ar, 33bl, 54br, 56al; Hutchison Library: 59ar; Kimball Morrison, South American Pictures: 18ar; Tony Morrison, South American Pictures: 13al, 13br, 15bc, `8cl, 27al, 27acl, 30ar, 33ar, 40bc, 42al, 43ac, 57ar; Museo Ciudad Mexico/Sapieha/e.t. archive: 12ac; Museo d'America, Madrid/Photo Scala: 6bl; Museum Für Vülkerkunde, Vienna: 49cr; Museum of

Mankind/ Bridgeman Art Library: (detail: Diego Rivera 'La Civilisation Zapotheque') 9bl, (detail, Diego Rivera 'Cultivation of Maize') 24bc, (detail: Diego Rivera 'The market of Tenochtitlan') 53bl, / e.t. archive 26c, (detail, Diego Rivera 'Tarascan Civilisation') 42cr; Peter Newark: 59acr; NHPA/Bernard: 13acl/Woodfall: 19b; Pate/Hutchison Library: 17acr; Private Collection/ Bridgeman Art Library: 6br; Rietberg Museum, Zurich: 10bl; Nick Saunders /Barbara heller: 18c, 19acl, 23al, 31ar, 63ar; Ronald Sheridan/Ancient Art and Architecture Collection: 51 acr; South American Pictures: 34c; University Museum, Cuzco/ e/t/ archive: 10ar; Werner Forman Archive/Antrhopology Museum, Veracruz: 9ar, Edward H. Merrin Gallery, New york: 45ar,/National Museum of Antrhopology, Mexico City: 53al; Michel Zabé: 30-31, 36bl, 47acl, 49c, 50al, 51ar, 52bl, 52c,/NMA, Mexico City: 29al.

Corbis: Archivo Iconografico, S.A. 67tr; Nathan Benn 66rr; Bettmann 67bl, 67br; Jonathan Blair 69br; Bohemian Nomad Picturemakers 64tl; Don Conrad 64bl; Sergio Dorantes 70-71; Macduff Everton 68-69; Randy Faris 66b; Kevin Fleming 69tl; Werner Forman 64-65, 70b; Angelo Hornak 65tr; Charles & Josette Lenars 67tl; Gianni Dagli

Orti 64br, 65cl, 69cl; Jose Luis Pelaez, Inc. 68tl; Bill Ross 71br; Kevin Schafer 65bc; Roman Soumar 68bl; Hubert Stadler 68cr; Linda Whitwam (c) CONACULTA-INAH-MEX Authorized reproduction by the Instituto Nacional de Antropologia e Historia 70tr; Getty Images: AFP 69bl

Every effort has been made to trace the copyright holders. The publisher apologizes for any unintentional omissions and would be pleased, in such cases, to add an acknowledgement in future editions.